# Mittens & Hats
## for Yarn Lovers
### Detailed Techniques for Knitting in the Round

Carri Hammett

Creative Publishing
international

**Creative Publishing international**

First published in the United States
of America by
Creative Publishing International, Inc.,
a member of
Quayside Publishing Group
400 First Avenue North
Suite 300
Minneapolis, MN 55401
1-800-328-3895
www.creativepub.com

ISBN-13: 9781589235755
ISBN-10: 1589235754

Printed in China
10 9 8 7 6 5 4 3

Library of Congress
Cataloging-in-Publication Data

Hammett, Carri, 1956-
  Mittens and hats for yarn lovers /
Carri Hammett.
      p. cm.
  Summary: "Beginner's guide to knitting
mittens and hats; includes instructions
for twenty-two projects"-- Provided by
publisher.
  ISBN-13: 978-1-58923-575-5 (hard
cover)
  ISBN-10: 1-58923-575-4 (hard cover)
  1. Knitting--Patterns. 2. Mittens. 3.
Hats.  I. Title.

  TT825.H25648 2011
  746.43'2--dc22

2010027951

Technical Editor: Karen Weiberg
Book Design: Mighty Media
Cover Design: Amy Hauge
Page Layout: Danielle Smith
Photographs: Corean Komarec

## DEDICATION

The book is dedicated to all my coworkers and customers at Coldwater Collaborative. Without you it wouldn't have been a community, with you it's a collaboration that has made us all better. A special thanks to Becky, Bridgit, Pam, and Robyn for your unfailing loyalty, hard work, creativity and support for all those years.

I wouldn't have been able to finish this book without the expert knitting of Becky, Bridgit, Pam, Robyn, and Suz. Thanks for all your hard work but most of all for telling me when I was wrong!

## YARN LIST

To purchase any of the yarns found in this book visit Carri's web site: www.coldwateryarn.com or stop in at your LYS!

For more information about the yarns used in the book, check these manufacturer's web sites:

| | |
|---|---|
| Berroco | www.berroco.com |
| Cascade Yarns | www.cascadeyarns.com |
| Classic Elite Yarns | www.classiceliteyarns.com |
| Crystal Palace Yarns | www.straw.com |
| Debbi Bliss | www.knittingfever.com |
| Dream in Color Yarn | www.dreamincoloryarn.com |
| The Fibre Company | www.thefibreco.com |
| Filatura di Crosa | www.tahkistacycharles.com |
| Frog Tree Yarns | www.frogtreeyarns.com |
| Hand Maiden Fine Yarn | www.handmaiden.ca |
| Lorna's Laces | www.lornaslaces.net |
| Malabrigo Yarn | www.malabrigoyarn.com |
| Misti Alpaca | www.mistialpaca.com |
| Nashua Handknits | www.westminsterfibers.com |
| Plymouth Yarn | www.plymouthyarn.com |
| Rowan | www.westminsterfibers.com |
| Shibui Knits | www.shibuiknits.com |
| Skacel Collection Inc. (Addi Turbo) | www.skacelknitting.com |
| Tahki Yarns | www.tahkistacycharles.com |

# Contents

# Introduction

Carri Hammett is the original owner of Coldwater Collaborative, a gem of a yarn shop in Excelsior, Minnesota. Since opening the shop in 2002 she has developed a loyal customer base from not only the Twin Cities but all over the world. Carri loves to collaborate both with her customers and her readers as together they express their love of knitting and expand their knitting knowledge and skill. She is also the author of *Scarves and Shawls for Yarn Lovers* and *Ready, Set, Knit Cables*.

Carri lives in Minnesota with her husband. She has three kids who live too far from home but at least they all know how to knit (she's still working on her husband to learn). Carri loves to hear from her readers. You can send her an email at carri@coldwateryarn.com.

I wrote a similar book to this one several years ago called *Scarves and Shawls for Yarn Lovers.* At the time yarn shops were awash in novelty yarns of every texture—ladder, ribbon, eyelash, fur, and sometimes a combination of all of those. During that time luxury fibers and hand-dyed yarns also became easily available. This fiber feast was the inspiration for a huge number of people to learn how to knit. The craft of knitting usually starts out with the simplest project, the scarf. The framework of a scarf can be used to explore different fibers for a long time, but eventually knitters become dissatisfied with making only scarves and want to learn how to make something new. Knitting a hat or a pair of mittens is the perfect way to expand one's skills, and I find that even the most experienced knitters rarely grow tired of making these small items. Both are finished quickly, require interesting skills, and are ideal to take along because of their small size.

As my customers' knitting skills have evolved so too has the selection of yarns I sell. While I still sell novelty yarn, it now takes up only a section, not half the shop. Different fibers and the interesting ways they can be combined has become one of the focal points of the yarn that is sold in my shop. Fibers that might once have been considered exotic, such as alpaca, merino wool, cashmere, silk, and bamboo, are now standard. Another focal point is color. Hand-dyed yarns and self-striping yarns continue to be important but the colors have become richer and more subtle, such as with semi-solid hand-dyed colors.

The popularity of yarns that are more simple yet elegant and the desire of my customers to expand their knitting skills are what inspired me to write this book. I not only want to give knitters the basic information and patterns they need to make mittens and hats, but I also hope they will use the skills they learn to create patterns of their own. Also, I've shared some of my favorite designs that I've developed for my customers over the past few years. You can take this book with you to any local yarn shop (LYS) and they will be able to help you find the yarns that are listed or similar yarns that you can substitute (especially if you live in a warmer climate and want to use cotton instead of wool). If you can't find the yarn at your LYS then check out my online shop at www.coldwateryarn.com.

## HOW TO USE THIS BOOK

You will find that this is part reference book and part design book. The very beginning of the book has an explanation of terms and techniques and useful information about things like gauge, reading patterns, tools, and yarn. In addition, there is a guide for using one long circular needle to make small-circumference items; a technique known as Magic Loop. The list of abbreviations is at the very back of the book so it can be quickly found. Since there is only so much that can be packed into any one book, I urge you to purchase a basic knitting reference to supplement the explanations I've provided.

Also in the front you will find a section each for hats and mittens. Each of those sections has four chapters. The first chapter is a basic, step-by-step photo guide for how to knit a hat or mittens. Second you will find a chapter called Extras, which will tell you how to vary the basic design. Next, you will find what is called the Power chapter, which gives you basic patterns in multiple gauges. At the end of each section you'll find the Gallery chapter, which shows examples of the different gauge patterns made from a variety of yarns and combinations of yarns.

The middle part of the book has my favorite section, Mighty Minis, with hats and mittens for babies. It's my favorite because baby items are so much fun and quick to make. The last section of the book is the Design Collection with many of my most unique and popular designs. Not only will you have the opportunity to explore the use of different yarns but the patterns offer a variety of techniques and skills for you to learn.

If you've never made a hat or mittens, then start with the Basics chapter and follow the step-by-step guide. Knitters of every skill level will find the Power chapter useful because it gives you the ability to use a wide range of yarns (a great way to diminish your stash). Hopefully every knitter will find inspiration in the one-of-a-kind patterns found in the rest of the book.

# Knit Basics

## Tools and Yarn

One of the great things about knitting is its underlying simplicity. You only need a few tools and some yarn to enjoy knitting.

### WHAT'S IN YOUR KNITTING BAG

When you are stocking your knitting bag, don't skimp on quality. Nothing is more frustrating than a poor quality circular needle, so please visit your local yarn shop (LYS) and let them help you stock your knitting bag. To make the items in this book you will need a 16" (41 cm) circular needle and double pointed needles in various sizes or, if desired, you can use 32" and 40" (81 and 101 cm) circular needles for mittens and hats (for the Magic Loop technique). In addition, you will need a blunt-end yarn needle, a cable needle, a tape measure, circular stitch markers, and a small stitch holder or some waste yarn. A knitting bag or basket is a great idea especially if you have a pet (cats love yarn balls and dogs adore chewing on bamboo needles). Finally you should have a few books in your bag; this one (of course), a good knitting reference book, and a notebook and row counter for keeping track of your knitting (unless you write it down you may forget what round you were on when the phone rang).

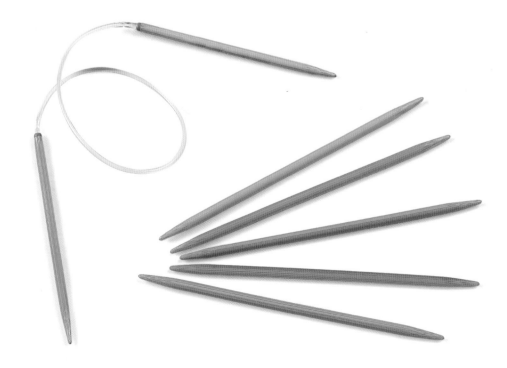

## WHAT ABOUT THE YARN?

All too often new customers visit my shop when they are frustrated with the quality of yarn they purchased somewhere else because they didn't want to spend too much money on yarn when they were 'just learning'. Nothing is more important than using high quality yarn, especially when you are learning a new skill. Notice I said high quality, not high price. You can buy a 200-yd skein of excellent wool yarn at your LYS for what you would spend on two small lattes.

So, look for good quality yarn that is either sold at your LYS or by a reputable online source and remember that cheaper isn't better!

If you're like just about every knitter I know, you have a stash of yarn at home. If you can't find the perfect pattern for a ball of yarn, then consider combining it with another orphan in your stash to make something completely different. Before jumping into combinations, let's define some yarn gauges:

## YARN COMBINATIONS

Open up your stash box and get creative with combinations. The best method for finding appealing combinations is to just put some yarns together and start swatching. Consult the guideline below as a starting point for combining yarn. See page 10 for more information about making a gauge swatch.

---

### GUIDE TO YARN COMBINATIONS

2 strands of fingering = 1 strand of DK

1 strand of fingering and
1 strand of sport = 1 strand of worsted

2 strands of worsted = 1 strand of chunky

1 strand of worsted and
1 strand of chunky = 1 strand of super bulky

---

### YARN GAUGES

| Yarn Type | Usual Gauge |
|---|---|
| Fingering | 7 or 8 sts per inch |
| Sport | 6 sts per inch |
| DK | 5½ sts per inch |
| Worsted | 5 sts per inch |
| Chunky | 3½ sts per inch |
| Super Bulky | 2½ sts per inch |
| *Note: 1" = 2.5 cm* | |

# Terms and Techniques

Throughout the book, you will find various knitting terms and techniques that may or may not be familiar to you. Refer to this section if you encounter an unfamiliar term or technique or if you need to refresh your memory on how to knit a particular stitch.

## GAUGE

The concept of making a gauge swatch is not popular with many knitters, but if you want your hat or mittens to turn out the way you expect, you must take the time to make a gauge swatch! If I could tell every knitter one thing about gauge, it's this: *you don't have to use the size needle that is called for in the pattern.* Every knitter is different; some are loose knitters (like me), some are tight knitters, and some knit at the same tension as that mysterious person who decided to specify a needle size on the yarn's ball band. Since I'm a loose knitter, I normally start my swatch with a needle that is at least one size smaller. The information on the yarn's ball band can provide helpful information about needle size in addition to what is specified in the pattern. *Remember this: It's not your job to change your knitting style, it's only your job to find the size needle that allows you to knit at the same gauge as the pattern.*

Generally, the gauge is specified for the main body of knitting on the item, and the first needle that is listed in the needle section is the size that is "recommended" to achieve that gauge. For instance on a hat, the gauge is for the stockinette stitch portion that is made after the ribbing is completed. If you use a needle that is different than the one specified in the pattern, then you will also need to change the needle size used for the ribbing as well. Generally this needle will be two sizes smaller. Once you find the size needle you need in order to achieve the correct gauge, then use a needle for the ribbing that is proportionally smaller. For instance, imagine working with a pattern that calls for a size 7 (4.5 mm) for the gauge swatch and 5 (3.75 mm) for the ribbing. If you find that you need a size 6 (4 mm) to achieve the gauge, then you will need a size 4 (3.5 mm) for the ribbing.

When knitting in the round it's a good idea to swatch in the round because the majority of your work will be in stockinette stitch (all knit), and most knitters work purl stitches at a different tension compared to knit stitches. I normally cast on 30 to 40 stitches and join them in the round for my swatch. I swap needles in and out until I feel I'm getting the correct gauge and *then I knit for a few more inches to be sure.*

## SLIPPING STITCHES

Unless otherwise stated, a stitch should be slipped as if to purl which maintains its orientation relative to the needle.

### SLIPPING KNITWISE AND PURLWISE

Slipping a stitch simply means moving it from the left needle to the right needle without knitting or purling it. A stitch is slipped knitwise by inserting the right needle from the front to the back (as if you were getting ready to knit) and then moving it to the right needle. A stitch is slipped purlwise by inserting the right needle from the back to the front (as if you were getting ready to purl) and then moving it to the right needle.

## WITH YARN IN FRONT (WYIF)
## WITH YARN IN BACK (WYIB)

These are terms often associated with slip stitch patterns and they simply refer to where the working yarn is when the stitch is slipped, either in front of the needle (wyif) or behind the needle (wyib).

# INCREASES
## LIFTED INCREASE (INC)

Tilt your work slightly so you can see the back side of the knitting. Use your right needle to lift up the loop from the stitch that's directly below the stitch on your left needle (1). Place this loop on your left needle (2) and knit into it (3) thereby adding an extra stitch.

1

2

3

## KNIT FRONT AND BACK (KF&B)

This is known as the bar increase because a small bar is formed on the right side of the knitting.

First knit in the usual way but don't take the new stitch off your left needle (4). Pivot the right needle to the back of the left needle and insert it knitwise (from front to back) into the back loop of the same stitch just worked. Make another stitch into the back loop (5). Slip the old stitch off the left needle. There are now two stitches in place of one.

4

5

## PURL FRONT AND BACK (PF&B)

First purl in the usual way but don't take the new stitch off the left needle. Keeping the working yarn in front, pivot the right needle to the back of the left needle and insert it purlwise (from back to front) into the back loop of the same stitch just worked (6). Make another purl stitch in the back loop. Slip the old stitch off the left needle. There are now two stitches in place of one.

6

### MAKE ONE (M1)

Several different versions of the make one increase are used in this book and they all have in common the fact that they make a stitch out of the horizontal bar or "ladder" that extends between every two stitches. The bar is picked up onto the left needle and then worked as a knit stitch or a purl stitch. The increase is caused to slant by how the bar is picked up, either from the front or the back. This type of increase leaves a tiny hole at the base of the new stitch.

### MAKE ONE LEFT (M1L)

Working from front to back, insert left needle under the horizontal bar between the stitch on the right needle and the stitch on the left needle (1). Knit this strand through the back loop to give it a twist (2).

### MAKE ONE RIGHT (M1R)

Working from back to front insert left needle under the horizontal bar between the stitch on the right needle and the stitch on the left needle. Knit this strand through the front loop to give it a twist.

### MAKE ONE RIGHT PURL (M1RP)

To work the same increase on the purl side insert the left needle from back to front under the horizontal bar and work a purl stitch through the front loop.

### YARNOVER (YO)

Bring yarn forward between needles and lay it over the right needle in a counter clockwise direction ending behind the needle. Knit the next stitch (3). Notice that the yarnover has made an extra loop on the right needle that will be worked as a stitch on the next row.

### MAKE ONE LEFT PURL (M1LP)

To work the same increase on the purl side, insert the left needle from front to back under the horizontal bar and work a purl stitch through the back loop.

### BACKWARD THUMB LOOP

This is essentially a cast-on that adds one or more stitches at the beginning of a row or to be used for shaping. Wrap the working yarn around left thumb from front to back and use your other fingers to hold the yarn end firmly against your palm (4). Insert the right needle upward into the loop, release it from your left thumb, and transfer the loop to the right needle (5).

## DECREASES

### KNIT TWO TOGETHER (K2TOG)

Insert the right needle knitwise into the next two stitches on the left needle. Knit these two stitches at the same time as if they were one stitch (6).

### KNIT THREE TOGETHER (K3TOG)

Work as for k2tog but insert right needle into next three stitches on left needle.

### PURL TWO TOGETHER (P2TOG)

Insert the right needle purlwise into the next two stitches on the left needle. Purl these two stitches at the same time as if they were one stitch (7).

### PURL THREE TOGETHER (P3TOG)

Work as for p2tog but insert right needle into next three stitches on left needle.

### SLIP, SLIP, KNIT (SSK)

This decrease is very similar to the k2tog except that the decrease is worked through the back loops of two stitches at a time. Working one at a time, slip two stitches knitwise to right needle (8). Insert the tip of the left needle into the front loops of these two stitches. Knit these stitches at the same time through the back loops as if they were one stitch (9).

### PASS SLIP STITCH OVER (PSSO)

Slip the first stitch on the left needle knitwise, then knit the next stitch on the left needle. Use the left needle tip to pick up the slipped stitch and pass it over the knit stitch just made and off the end of the right needle.

## CABLES AND TWIST STITCHES

### FOUR-STITCH RIGHT KNIT CROSS (4-ST RKC)

Slip next 2 stitches purlwise to cable needle and hold at back of work (1), knit next 2 stitches from left needle, knit 2 stitches from cable needle (2).

### SIX-STITCH RIGHT KNIT CROSS (6-ST RKC)

Slip next 3 stitches purlwise to cable needle and hold at back of work, knit next 3 stitches from left needle, knit 3 stitches from cable needle.

### TWO-STITCH RIGHT TWIST (2-ST RT)

K2tog but don't take the stitches off the left needle, there will be one new stitch on the right needle (3). Insert right needle into first stitch on left needle (4), knit it and then remove both stitches from left needle. Two new stitches have been formed on the right needle and the stitch count remains the same.

3

1

4

2

## OTHER TECHNIQUES

### PICK UP AND KNIT

Stitches are added to an already knitted edge by picking up and knitting. This is a confusing term; you aren't actually *knitting* the stitch as you pick it up. Rather, the stitch is picked up *knitwise* onto the right needle to be knit on the next round or row. Working from the

right side, insert the right needle from front to back going under two strands* along the edge (5). Wrap the yarn around the needle as if you were knitting and pull a loop through and onto the right needle (6). Continue in this manner until the required stitches have been added.
*On occasion when picking up stitches for mittens, only one strand will be available.

## WORKING IN THE ROUND— STOCKINETTE STITCH AND GARTER STITCH

Working in the round differs from knitting back and forth. To work stockinette stitch in the round, every round is knit. To work garter stitch in the round, a purl round is alternated with a knit round. For more information about knitting these two stitches in the round see Hat Extras, page 24.

## READING PATTERNS

You will find two special symbols in patterns, * * and [ ]. Both are used to indicate a repeat in the round. Generally directions between asterisks such as *k2, p2* are repeated over and over to the end of the round or until a specified number of stitches remain. Likewise, directions between brackets are repeated a number of times before proceeding to another set of directions on that round. For instance, [k2, p2] twice means that you will k2, p2, k2, p2 before working the next set of directions in the round.

## MULTIPLE SIZES

Because most of the patterns are written for a range of sizes, it will be necessary to determine which directions apply to the size you are making. In most cases, a chart will be shown which defines the dimensions of a particular size and for the sake of simplicity gives that size a name; Size 1, Size 2, Size 3, etc. Following the chart you will find the specification of how the directions for the sizes will be shown in the pattern using one or more sets of parentheses. For example, the Hat Power 5.0, page 27 is written in four sizes. The directions are shown in this order: Size 1 (Size 2, Size 3, Size 4). The first line of the pattern reads: *Cast on 88 (96, 104, 112) sts.* If you're making size 3, which is the middle direction inside the parentheses, then you will cast on 104 stitches.

When working from a pattern with a large number of sizes, it's a good idea to photocopy the pattern before you start so you can highlight all the directions applying to the size you are making. In defense of hard-working authors and designers, I must implore you to only make copies from a book for your own use and not share with others.

You will notice that the some of the rows have a lot of information in terms of which size the directions apply to. Please pay careful attention (this is where highlighting is so helpful). If the row doesn't specify a particular size then you can assume that it applies to all sizes.

# MAGIC LOOP

Sarah Hauschka wrote a little gem of a book called *The Magic Loop* (available from Fiber Trends, www.fibertrends.com). In the book, she explains how to use a long circular needle to knit small-circumference items (like socks) in the round. The Magic Loop method is just as useful for hats and mittens and the step-by-step directions below show you how to make a pair of mittens.

### WHY USE MAGIC LOOP?

I have a confession to make: I use the Magic Loop method on most of my mitten and hat knitting. I like the fact that I only need to keep track of one needle instead of four or five double-pointed needles (you can knit as few as four stitches using Magic Loop). Also, when I have to set my knitting aside, I simply pull the needles so that all the knitting rests on the cables so I don't have to worry about dropped stitches. The most important reason is the arthritis in my thumbs. The needle shanks on a 16" (40 cm) circular needle are very short compared to longer circular needles and it hurts my hands to hold onto them. I simply find longer circular needles much more comfortable to use.

### BEFORE GETTING STARTED

There are just a few more details to point out before you learn the basics. Choose high-quality circular needles with supple, flexible cable (I use Addi Turbos, available at your LYS). When making hats, the length of the needle from tip to tip should be at least 40" (102 cm) long. When making a pair of mittens you might find a 32" (81 cm) long needle easier to use because you won't have to pull as much cable but the 40" (102 cm) will work just fine.

My method of getting started is different than what is shown in *The Magic Loop*. I like to place the beginning of the round in the middle of the needle instead of the tip because I think it's easier to pull the joining stitches together without a gap.

### MAKING A MITTEN
### USING THE MAGIC LOOP METHOD

Using the smaller circular needle cast on the number of stitches as called for in the pattern. Slide the stitches so that all of them are off the needle shaft and on the cable (1). As with any other circular knitting it is important to make sure that the stitches are not twisted so make sure that the bumps at the bottom of the stitches are lined up facing the center of the arc formed by the cable. The last stitch that was cast on will be closest to the right needle and the first stitch will be closest to the left needle.

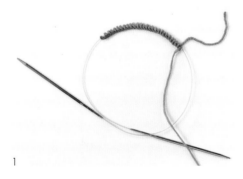

1

Moving from the right to the left, pinch the cable at the point which is past approximately 25% of the stitches, and pull out a loop of cable (2). Continuing to work from the right to the left, pinch the cable again at the point which is past about 75% of the stitches, and pull out a second loop.

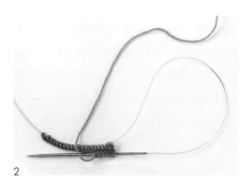

2

Enlarge the loops enough so that the first several stitches can be slid to the right needle tip and the last several stitches can be slid to the left needle tip (3).

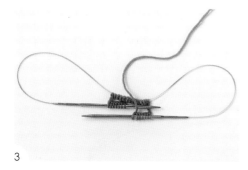

3

Half of the stitches remain on the cable while 25% are on each needle. The working yarn is draped up and over the cable ready to form the first knit stitch. The bumps at the bottom of the stitches are still oriented toward the center and not twisted. Insert the right needle into the first loop on the left needle and form the first stitch pulling the working yarn tightly to close the gap between the two needles (4).

4

Continue working across the left needle until it is emptied of stitches. At this point, half the stitches are on the front needle and half are on the back needle.

Turn the work so the needle with the unworked stitches is in front and pull the cable (or push the needle if it's more comfortable) so the stitches move to the tip of the needle (the needle with the working yarn attached is in the back) (5).

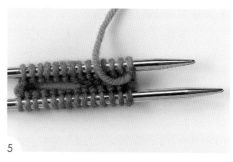

5

Using your right hand, pull out the back needle (the one attached to the working yarn), letting the back stitches move onto the cable. Allow the cable to form a long enough loop so that you can use the back (right) needle to knit across the stitches on the front needle (6).

6

Use the right needle to work the stitches off the left needle. Once again the knitting needs to be turned, the cables pulled through to form new loops, and the back needle brought to the front needle to start a new round. On your first few rounds you may notice a gap in your knitting where the yarn is stretched a bit between the front and back needles but this will disappear after several rounds.

You can place a marker to indicate the beginning of the round (found just after the tail that is left from the cast-on) when the needles are first joined or wait until the first round is completed.

Once the cuff is finished you must change to the larger needle. Do so by using the larger needle to knit the stitches off the front (smaller) needle. Turn the knitting around and pull the smaller needle so that the stitches move onto the smaller needle shank. Making the first loop with the larger needle, knit across the second set of stitches. Now, continue knitting as before using the larger needle.

All of the gusset increases should be made within just one needle's group of stitches. The cable loop should not be formed in the middle of the gusset (7).

9

7

When reaching the point at which the stitches are decreased to shape the mitten tip you can continue using the same needle as this technique works just as well for a small number of stitches (8).

8

The Magic Loop method can also be used to complete the thumb by dividing the stitches between the two needles. Put a few more stitches on the front needle to allow space on the back needle for picking up stitches over the gap on the gusset (9).

## MAKING A HAT
## USING THE MAGIC LOOP METHOD

Getting started making a hat using a long circular needle is similar to a mitten. The only difference is that you need to use a needle that is at least 40" (100 cm) long; a shorter length will put too much pressure on the stitches between the front and back needles and will cause a gap. As before, cast on all the stitches to the smaller needle (if the hat begins with ribbing). For the first round, place the beginning of the round in the middle of the front set of stitches, dividing the stitches with approximately 25% on each needle and 50% on the back cable.

Since this method can be used with a very small number of stitches it is not necessary to transfer the stitches to double-pointed needles when making the decreases for the crown.

# Hats

## Hat Basics

The essence of simplicity is a roll-brim hat made out of medium weight yarn. Traditionally called worsted weight, it is the most common thickness found in yarn shops. If this is the first hat you are making then choose a high-quality wool yarn such as the one shown. You'll find that wool is far more forgiving for a beginning knitter. Its natural elasticity not only makes it easier to maintain even knitting tension, but causes the hat to spring back into its original shape after being stretched over a person's head.

## HAT BASICS: Size, Finished Dimensions, and Yardage

| | To Fit Size | Finished Hat Circumference | Short Hat Height* | Tall Hat Height* | Approximate Yardage Required |
|---|---|---|---|---|---|
| **Size 1** | 2 to 4 year | 17½" (44 cm) | 6½" (17 cm) | 7½" (19 cm) | 100 to 120 yd (91 to 110 m) |
| **Size 2** | 5 year to Adult Small | 19" (48 cm) | 7¼" (18 cm) | 8½" (22 cm) | 115 to 140 yd (105 to 128 m) |
| **Size 3** | Adult Medium | 21" (53 cm) | 8" (20 cm) | 9½" (24 cm) | 130 to 160 yd (119 to 146 m) |
| **Size 4** | Adult Large | 22½" (57 cm) | 9" (23 cm) | 10½" (27 cm) | 180 to 220 yd (166 to 202 m) |

Directions will be shown in the pattern as follows: Size 1 (Size 2, Size 3, Size 4)
*For explanation of hat height see pages 24 and 25

## STEP-BY-STEP GUIDE FOR KNITTING A HAT

*The step-by-step guide is intended for the knitter who has never made a hat. Knitting directions are written in plain text, followed by further explanation in italics.*

Because this pattern is written for a range of sizes it will be necessary to determine which directions apply to the size you are making. Below the chart you will find the specification of how the directions for the different sizes will be shown in the pattern using one or more sets of parentheses. For example, this pattern is written in four sizes. The directions are shown in this order: Size 1 (Size 2, Size 3, Size 4). The first line of the pattern reads: Cast on 88 (96, 104, 112) sts. If you're making size 3, which is the middle direction inside the parentheses, then you will cast on 104 stitches. It's a good idea to photocopy the pattern before you start so you can highlight all the directions applying to the size you are making.

### CAST ON STITCHES AND BEGIN KNITTING
Using the circular needle, cast on 88 (96, 104, 112) stitches. Place beginning-of-round (BOR) marker and join in the round, being careful not to twist.

*There's nothing complicated about joining your knitting in the round except that you need to pay attention on this first step where it says, "being careful not to twist". It's important that your chain of cast-on stitches does not twist or spiral around the needle. To avoid this problem, always make sure that the bumps at the bottom of the stitches are lined up facing the center of the circle formed by the needle.*

### GAUGE

20 sts = 4" (10 cm) in stockinette stitch

**Important:** Make a gauge swatch before you start knitting. It's the only way to make sure the hat will turn out the way you expect. (See page 10.)

### YARN

Medium weight smooth yarn; the approximate yardage for each size is shown in the chart at left.

Shown: Cascade Yarns 220 Wool, 100% wool; 220 yd (201 m) per 3.5 oz (100 g) skein

### NEEDLES AND NOTIONS

US size 7 (4.5 mm) 16" (41 cm) circular needle or size required to achieve gauge

US size 7 (4.5 mm) double-pointed needles or size required to achieve gauge

Circular stitch marker

Yarn needle for weaving in ends

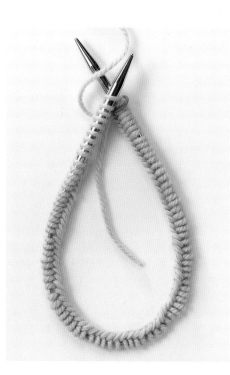

The first stitch that was cast on is on the left needle and the last stitch, connected to the working yarn, is on the right needle. Before making the first stitch, slip a stitch marker over the right needle, now insert the right needle into the left stitch and use the working yarn to begin knitting around the needle.

Pull the yarn tightly when working the very first stitch to avoid a gap and knit completely around the stitches until you reach the marker. The marker indicates the beginning of the round (BOR) and it should be slipped to the right needle before each subsequent round. Every time you work around the stitches and back to the BOR marker, one round has been completed.

### HAT BODY

Work in stockinette stitch (knit all stitches) until the length from the cast-on row is 6" (6½", 7¼", 8") [15 (16.5, 18.5, 20) cm]. The rolled edge will need to e unrolled in order to measure the length accurately.

### SHAPE TOP

The stitches are divided into eight wedges and gradually decreased to form a tapered shape. Notice that the larger sizes require more rows to decrease their greater number of stitches. If you are making one of the smaller sizes, then skip the rows that don't apply to your hat. For instance, if you are making a Size 3, then skip the directions for rounds 1 and 2 and begin the decreases for your hat on round 3.

Asterisks * are used to designate the beginning and end of the decrease directions. Repeat the directions between the asterisks over and over until the end of the round is reached. Some knitters find it easier to keep track of the decrease sections by placing a marker at the beginning of each section (the directions enclosed by asterisks). Just make sure your decrease markers are a different color from the BOR marker.

When the number of stitches has decreased to the point where they can no longer be easily stretched around the circumference of the circular needle, you must transfer them to double-pointed needles (DPNs) (1). The easiest way to do that is simply knit off the circular needle and onto the DPNs. Because you are working eight decrease wedges it works well to place a quarter of the stitches on each of four DPNs with one of the k2tog decreases ending up at the end of each needle. It's best to place the BOR marker in the middle of one of the needles, so start to transfer the stitches to the first DPN at the beginning of the last decrease wedge before the end of the round. This will place the last wedge, the BOR marker, and the first wedge all on the same needle.

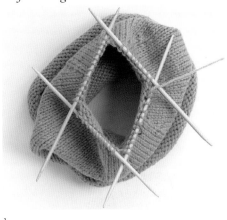

1

Once all the stitches are transferred to the four DPNs, the fifth needle will be used for knitting the stitches (2). Don't try to hold all the needles at once; just hold the two needles you are working on and let the other needles hang in place. Work your way through the stitches in the round just as if you are still using a circular needle.

2

After working stockinette to desired length (see page 21), continue as follows:

**Round 1 for size 4 only:** *Knit 12, k2tog*; repeat from * to * to end of round—104 sts remain.

**Round 2 for size 4 only:** Knit.

**Round 3 for sizes 3 and 4 only:** *Knit 11, k2tog*; repeat from * to * to end of round—96 sts remain.

**Round 4 for sizes 3 and 4 only:** Knit.

**Round 5 for sizes 2, 3, and 4 only:** *Knit 10, k2tog*; repeat from * to * to end of round—88 sts remain.

**Round 6 for sizes 2, 3, and 4 only:** Knit. From this point, all four sizes are worked identically.

**Round 7:** *Knit 9, k2tog*; repeat from * to * to end of round—80 sts remain.

**Round 8:** Knit.

**Round 9:** *Knit 8, k2tog*; repeat from * to * to end of round—72 sts remain.

**Round 10:** Knit.

**Round 11:** *Knit 7, k2tog*; repeat from * to * to end of round—64 sts remain.

**Round 12:** Knit.

**Round 13:** *Knit 6, k2tog*; repeat from * to * to end of round—56 sts remain.

**Round 14:** Knit.

**Round 15:** *Knit 5, k2tog*; repeat from * to * to end of round—48 sts remain.

**Round 16:** Knit.

**Round 17:** *Knit 4, k2tog*; repeat from * to * to end of round—40 sts remain.

**Round 18:** Knit.

**Round 19:** *Knit 3, k2tog*; repeat from * to * to end of round—32 sts remain.

**Round 20:** Knit.

**Round 21:** *Knit 2, k2tog*; repeat from * to * to end of round—24 sts remain.

**Round 22:** Knit.

**Round 23:** *Knit 1, k2tog*; repeat from * to * to end of round—16 sts remain.

**Round 24:** Knit.

**Round 25:** *K2tog*; repeat from * to * to end of round—8 sts remain.

To finish the hat, remove the marker and cut the yarn leaving a tail at least 8" (20 cm) long. Using a yarn needle, thread the tail through the remaining stitches and pass through the hole in the top of the hat to the inside. Pull the tail firmly to close the hole and weave the ends into the stitches on the inside of the hat to secure.

# Hat Extras

Once you've learned the basics of making a simple roll-brim hat then you'll want to vary the design by changing elements like the edge treatment and the height of the hat.

## CHANGING THE EDGE

Stockinette stitch curls whether it is used on the bottom of a sweater or to start a hat. On a hat, that curled edge is known as a roll-brim.

When you are making a flat item in stockinette stitch then the right side, the *public* side, is worked in knit stitch and the wrong side, the *private* side, is worked in purl stitch. However, when knitting in the round, for instance on a hat, you are always working on the outside (the public side). To make stockinette stitch in the round, **every** round is worked in knit stitch.

If you don't want a roll-brim at the beginning of a hat, then you must first work some rounds using a stitch that doesn't curl. The most popular edge treatment for a hat is ribbing but seed stitch and garter stitch also work well. Shown above are two hats that are basically identical except for the beginning rows. The hat on the left is a roll-brim and the hat on the right begins with four rows of knit 2, purl 2 ribbing. For more ideas about edge treatments see Mitten Extras on page 46.

## CHANGING THE HEIGHT

Short hat or tall hat? The height of a hat can cause a remarkable change in its appearance. The shaping of the crown is normally set by the pattern but you can vary the distance between the bottom edge and the point where the decreases for the shaping begin. In the Hat Power section, the patterns specify two different heights, *Short* and *Tall*. Neither one of the hat heights includes any additional length that might be added to accommodate what might curl upward for a roll-brim hat. If you are making a roll-brim hat, then add 1" to 2" (2.5 to 5 cm) to the total knitted length (heavier yarn requires a longer length to roll). This additional length won't make the hat any longer when worn but will be taken up by the decorative roll brim.

The short height gives a fit that is often referred to as a skully or a beanie. This style fits snugly to the top of the head and covers most of the ears.

The tall height still covers the ears but gives the hat some fullness, or poufiness, at the top. In the photos below, the woman is wearing a short hat (Hat Nation, page 135) and the girl is wearing the tall version of the Color Therapy Hat (page 106).

Another way to change the look of a hat is to make a long ribbing section at the beginning, 4" to 5" (10 to 13 cm) for an average adult. When the ribbing is folded in half into a cuff the hat becomes what is known as a watch cap. Add the desired height of the visible portion of the cuff to the total height specified by the pattern before shaping begins. For example, if a hat pattern calls for shaping to begin at 6" (15 cm), I would make the length 8½" (21.5 cm) instead, to give a 2½" (6 cm) cuff. I would work the first 5" (12.5 cm) in ribbing and the last 3½" (9 cm) in stockinette stitch before shaping begins (see page 36). I normally make both the visible and hidden portions of the cuff in ribbing.

A popular style being worn by younger people and hip movie stars is the slouch hat. To make a hat with a long "slouchy" portion extending past the top of the head, make the length about 3" (7.5 cm) longer than what is specified for the tall height in the Hat Power section. As you can see from the photo below, even a baby can wear a hip slouch hat (see Shout Out Loud Hat, page 78).

# Hat Power

You can choose any yarn to knit a hat. In this section, the basic hat pattern is given in various gauges. Follow the *Hat Power* instructions that are written for the gauge recommended on the yarn label. It is important to knit a gauge swatch before you begin to be sure you are knitting at the same tension as shown on the label (for more information on gauge, see page 10).

Also, this pattern gives directions for a ribbed edge instead of a roll brim. As discussed in Hat Extras (page 22), you can vary the look of your hat by how you knit the beginning edge (the brim) and also by how high you make the hat. This pattern tells you when to begin shaping for either a short height or a tall height hat.

## HAT POWER 5.5: Size, Finished Dimensions, and Yardage

| | To Fit Size | Finished Hat Circumference | Short Hat Height | Tall Hat Height | Approximate Yardage Required |
|---|---|---|---|---|---|
| Size 1 | 2 to 4 year | 17½" (43 cm) | 6½" (17 cm) | 7½" (19 cm) | 120 to 145 yd (10 to 133 m) |
| Size 2 | 5 year to Adult Small | 19" (48 cm) | 7¼" (18 cm) | 8½" (22 cm) | 140 to 170 yd (128 to 155 m) |
| Size 3 | Adult Medium | 20½" (52 cm) | 8" (20 cm) | 9½" (24 cm) | 160 to 200 yd (146 to 183 m) |
| Size 4 | Adult Large | 22" (56 cm) | 9" (23 cm) | 10½" (27 cm) | 220 to 270 yd (201 to 247 m) |

*Directions will be shown in the pattern as follows: Size 1 (Size 2, Size 3, Size 4)*

## HAT POWER 5.5
### 5½ STITCHES = 1 INCH (2.5 CM)

**CAST ON STITCHES AND BEGIN KNITTING**
Cast on 96 (104, 112, 120) stitches. Choose an edge style. Use the larger needle if you plan to make a roll brim hat in stockinette stitch (knit every stitch). Use the smaller needle if you plan to make the bottom edge in ribbing or garter stitch. Place BOR marker and join in the round being careful not to twist (see page 20).

**RIBBED EDGE**
**Round 1:** *K2, p2*; repeat from * to * to end of round.

Repeat Round 1 until ribbing is desired length from cast on edge. Change to larger needle and continue in stockinette stitch (knit every stitch).

**GARTER STITCH EDGE**
**Round 1:** Knit.
**Round 2:** Purl.
Repeat Rounds 1 and 2 until the garter stitch section is desired length from cast on edge. Change to larger needle and continue in stockinette stitch (knit every stitch).

## ROLL BRIM

Use the larger circular needle and begin knitting in stockinette stitch (knit every stitch) immediately.

## HAT BODY

Continue working in stockinette stitch until the length from the cast on row is:

- 4¼" (4¾", 5¼", 6")
  [11 (12, 13.5, 15) cm] for Short Hat
- 5¼" (6", 6¾", 7½")
  [13.5 (15, 17, 19) cm] for Tall Hat
- For a roll-brim add approximately 1" (2.5 cm) extra to the desired length above (the rolled edge will need to be unrolled in order to measure the length accurately).

## SHAPE TOP

Work decreases to shape the crown of the hat. Notice that the larger sizes require more rows to decrease their greater number of stitches. If you are making one of the smaller sizes then skip the rows that don't apply to your hat size. Change to double pointed needles when the stitches will no longer fit comfortably around the circular needle.

**Round 1 for size 4 only:** *Knit 13, k2tog*; repeat from * to * to end of round—112 sts remain.

**Round 2 for size 4 only:** Knit.

**Round 3 for sizes 3 and 4 only:** *Knit 12, k2tog*; repeat from * to * to end of round—104 sts remain.

**Round 4 for sizes 3 and 4 only:** Knit.

**Round 5 for sizes 2, 3, and 4 only:** *Knit 11, k2tog*; repeat from * to * to end of round—96 sts remain.

**Round 6 for sizes 2, 3, and 4 only:** Knit.

From this point, all four sizes are worked identically:

**Round 7:** *Knit 10, k2tog*; repeat from * to * to end of round—88 sts remain.

**Round 8:** Knit.

**Round 9:** *Knit 9, k2tog*; repeat from * to * to end of round—80 sts remain.

**Round 10:** Knit.

**Round 11:** *Knit 8, k2tog*; repeat from * to * to end of round—72 sts remain.

**Round 12:** Knit.

**Round 13:** *Knit 7, k2tog*; repeat from * to * to end of round—64 sts remain.

**Round 14:** Knit.

**Round 15:** *Knit 6, k2tog*; repeat from * to * to end of round—56 sts remain.

**Round 16:** Knit.

**Round 17:** *Knit 5, k2tog*; repeat from * to * to end of round—48 sts remain.

**Round 18:** Knit.

**Round 19:** *Knit 4, k2tog*; repeat from * to * to end of round—40 sts remain.

**Round 20:** Knit.

**Round 21:** *Knit 3, k2tog*; repeat from * to * to end of round—32 sts remain.

**Round 22:** Knit.

**Round 23:** *Knit 2, k2tog*; repeat from * to * to end of round—24 sts remain.
**Round 24:** Knit.
**Round 25:** *Knit 1, k2tog*; repeat from * to * to end of round—16 sts remain.
**Round 26:** Knit.
**Round 27:** *K2tog*; repeat from * to * to end of round—8 sts remain.

To finish the hat, cut the yarn leaving a tail at least 8" (20.3 cm) long. Using a yarn needle thread the tail through the remaining stitches and pass through the hole in the top of the hat to the inside. Pull the tail firmly to close the hole and weave the ends into the stitches on the inside of the hat to secure.

### HAT POWER 5.0: Size, Finished Dimensions, and Yardage

| | To Fit Size | Finished Hat Circumference | Short Hat Height | Tall Hat Height | Approximate Yardage Required |
|---|---|---|---|---|---|
| **Size 1** | 2 to 4 year | 17½" (44 cm) | 6½" (17 cm) | 7½" (19 cm) | 100 to 120 yd (91 to 110 m) |
| **Size 2** | 5 year to Adult Small | 19" (48 cm) | 7¼" (18 cm) | 8½" (22 cm) | 115 to 140 yd (105 to 128 m) |
| **Size 3** | Adult Medium | 21" (53 cm) | 8" (20 cm) | 9½" (24 cm) | 130 to 160 yd (119 to 146 m) |
| **Size 4** | Adult Large | 22½" (57 cm) | 9" (23 cm) | 10½" (27 cm) | 180 to 220 yd (166 to 202 m) |

*Directions will be shown in the pattern as follows: Size 1 (Size 2, Size 3, Size 4)*

## HAT POWER 5.0
### 5 STITCHES = 1 INCH (2.5 CM)

This is essentially the same pattern as the one used in Hat Basics (page 20) but without the longer explanations.

### CAST ON STITCHES AND BEGIN KNITTING
Cast on 88 (96, 104, 112). Choose an edge style. Use the larger needle to make a roll brim hat in stockinette stitch (knit every stitch). Use the smaller needle to make the bottom edge in ribbing or garter stitch. Place BOR marker and join in the round being careful not to twist (see page 20).

### RIBBED EDGE
**Round 1:** *K2, p2*; repeat from * to * to end of round.

Repeat round 1 until ribbing is desired length from cast on edge. Change to larger needle and continue in stockinette stitch (knit every stitch).

### GARTER STITCH EDGE
**Round 1:** Knit.
**Round 2:** Purl.

Repeat rounds 1 and 2 until the garter stitch section is desired length from cast on edge. Change to larger needle and continue in stockinette stitch (knit every stitch).

### ROLL BRIM
Use the larger circular needle and begin knitting in stockinette stitch (knit every stitch) immediately.

## HAT BODY

Continue working in stockinette stitch until the length from the cast on row is:

- 4¼" (4¾", 5¼", 6")
  [11 (12, 13.5, 15) cm] for short hat
- 5¼" (6", 6¾", 7½")
  [13.5 (15, 17, 19) cm] for tall hat
- For a roll-brim add approximately 1" (2.5 cm) extra to the desired length above (unroll the edge to measure accurately).

## SHAPE TOP

Work decreases to shape the crown of the hat. Notice that the larger sizes require more rows to decrease their greater number of stitches. If you are making one of the smaller sizes then skip the rows that don't apply to your hat size. Change to double pointed needles when the stitches will no longer fit comfortably around the circular needle.

**Round 1 for size 4 only:** *Knit 12, k2tog*; repeat from * to * to end of round—104 sts remain.

**Round 2 for size 4 only:** Knit.

**Round 3 for sizes 3 and 4 only:** *Knit 11, k2tog*; repeat from * to * to end of round—96 sts remain.

**Round 4 for sizes 3 and 4 only:** Knit.

**Round 5 for sizes 2, 3, and 4 only:** *Knit 10, k2tog*; repeat from * to * to end of round—88 sts remain.

**Round 6 for sizes 2, 3, and 4 only:** Knit.

From this point, all four sizes are worked identically:

**Round 7:** *Knit 9, k2tog*; repeat from * to * to end of round—80 sts remain.

**Round 8:** Knit.

**Round 9:** *Knit 8, k2tog*; repeat from * to * to end of round—72 sts remain.

**Round 10:** Knit.

**Round 11:** *Knit 7, k2tog*; repeat from * to * to end of round—64 sts remain.

**Round 12:** Knit.

**Round 13:** *Knit 6, k2tog*; repeat from * to * to end of round—56 sts remain.

**Round 14:** Knit.

**Round 15:** *Knit 5, k2tog*; repeat from * to * to end of round—48 sts remain.

**Round 16:** Knit.

**Round 17:** *Knit 4, k2tog*; repeat from * to * to end of round—40 sts remain.

**Round 18:** Knit.

**Round 19:** *Knit 3, k2tog*; repeat from * to * to end of round—32 sts remain.

**Round 20:** Knit.

**Round 21:** *Knit 2, k2tog*; repeat from * to * to end of round—24 sts remain.
**Round 22:** Knit.
**Round 23:** *Knit 1, k2tog*; repeat from * to * to end of round—16 sts remain.
**Round 24:** Knit.
**Round 25:** *K2tog*; repeat from * to * to end of round—8 sts remain.

To finish the hat, cut the yarn leaving a tail at least 8" (20.3 cm) long. Using a yarn needle thread the tail through the remaining stitches and pass through the hole in the top of the hat to the inside. Pull the tail firmly to close the hole and weave the ends into the stitches on the inside of the hat to secure.

---

### HAT POWER 3.5: Size, Finished Dimensions, and Yardage

|  | To Fit Size | Finished Hat Circumference | Short Hat Height | Tall Hat Height | Approximate Yardage Required |
|---|---|---|---|---|---|
| Size 1 | 2 to 4 year | 18" (46 cm) | 6½" (17 cm) | 7½" (19 cm) | 70 to 85 yd (64 to 78 m) |
| Size 2 | 5 year to Adult Small | 19½" (50 cm) | 7¼" (18 cm) | 8½" (22 cm) | 90 to 110 yd (82 to 101 m) |
| Size 3 | Adult Medium | 20½" (52 cm) | 8" (20 cm) | 9½" (24 cm) | 105 to 130 yd (96 to 119 m) |
| Size 4 | Adult Large | 23" (58 cm) | 9" (23 cm) | 10½" (27 cm) | 130 to 160 yd (119 to 146 m) |

*Directions will be shown in the pattern as follows: Size 1 (Size 2, Size 3, Size 4)*

---

## HAT POWER 3.5
### 3½ STITCHES = 1 INCH (2.5 CM)

### CAST ON STITCHES AND BEGIN KNITTING
Cast on 64 (68, 72, 80). Choose an edge style. Use the larger needle if you plan to make a roll-brim hat in stockinette stitch (knit every stitch). Use the smaller needle to make the bottom edge in ribbing or garter stitch. Place BOR marker and join in the round being careful not to twist (see page 20).

### RIBBED EDGE
**Round 1:** *K2, p2*; repeat from * to * to end of round.

Repeat round 1 until ribbing is desired length from cast-on edge. Change to larger needle and continue in stockinette stitch (knit every stitch).

### GARTER STITCH EDGE
**Round 1:** Knit.
**Round 2:** Purl.

Repeat rounds 1 and 2 until the garter stitch section is desired length from cast-on edge. Change to larger needle and continue in stockinette stitch (knit every stitch).

### ROLL-BRIM
Use the larger circular needle and begin knitting in stockinette stitch (knit every stitch) immediately.

## GAUGE

14 sts and 22 rows = 4" (10 cm) in stockinette stitch

## YARN

Bulky weight yarn; the approximate yardage for each size is shown in the chart at left.

## NEEDLES AND NOTIONS

US size 10½ (6.5 mm) 16" (41 cm) circular needle or size required to achieve gauge

US size 9 (5.5 mm) 16" (41 cm) circular needle (or two sizes smaller than size used to achieve gauge) to make an edge of ribbing or garter stitch

US size 10½ (6.5 mm) double-pointed needles or size required to achieve gauge

Optional Magic Loop: above needle sizes in a circular needle at least 40" (101 cm) long

Circular stitch marker

Yarn needle for weaving in ends

## HAT BODY

Continue working in stockinette stitch until the length from the cast-on row is:

- 4¼" (4¾", 5¼", 6") [11 (12, 13.5, 15) cm] for short hat
- 5¼" (6", 6¾", 7½") [13.5 (15, 17, 19) cm] for tall hat
- For a roll-brim add approximately 1" (2.5 cm) extra to the desired length above (unroll the edge to measure accurately).

## SHAPE TOP

Work decreases to shape the crown of the hat. Notice that the larger sizes require more rows to decrease their greater number of stitches. If you are one of the smaller sizes then skip the rows that don't apply to your hat size. Change to DPNs when the stitches will no longer fit comfortably around the circular needle.

**Round 1 for size 4 only:** *Knit 8, k2tog*; repeat from * to * to end of round—72 sts remain.

**Round 2 for size 4 only:** Knit.

**Round 3 for sizes 3 and 4 only:** *Knit 7, k2tog*; repeat from * to * to end of round—64 sts remain.

**Round 4 for sizes 3 and 4 only:** Knit.

**Round 4 for size 2 only:** *Knit 15, k2tog*; repeat from * to * to end of round—64 sts remain.

From this point, all four sizes are worked identically:

**Round 5:** *Knit 6, k2tog*; repeat from * to * to end of round—56 sts remain.

**Round 6:** Knit.

**Round 7:** *Knit 5, k2tog*; repeat from * to * to end of round—48 sts remain.

**Round 8:** Knit.

**Round 9:** *Knit 4, k2tog*; repeat from * to * to end of round—40 sts remain.

**Round 10:** Knit.

**Round 11:** *Knit 3, k2tog*; repeat from * to * to end of round—32 sts remain.

**Round 12:** Knit.

**Round 13:** *Knit 2, k2tog*; repeat from * to * to end of round—24 sts remain.

**Round 14:** Knit.

**Round 15:** *Knit 1, k2tog*; repeat from * to * to end of round—16 sts remain.

**Round 16:** Knit.

**Round 17:** *K2tog*; repeat from * to * to end of round—8 sts remain.

To finish the hat, cut the yarn, leaving a tail at least 8" (20 cm) long. Using a yarn needle, thread the tail through the remaining stitches and pass through the hole in the top of the hat to the inside. Pull the tail firmly to close the hole and weave the ends into the stitches on the inside of the hat to secure.

## HAT POWER 2.5: Size, Finished Dimensions, and Yardage

| | To Fit Size | Finished Hat Circumference | Short Hat Height | Tall Hat Height | Approximate Yardage Required |
|---|---|---|---|---|---|
| Size 1 | 2 to 4 year | 17½" (45 cm) | 6½" (17 cm) | 7½" (19 cm) | 40 to 55 yd (37 to 50 m) |
| Size 2 | 5 year to Adult Small | 19" (48 cm) | 7¼" (18 cm) | 8½" (22 cm) | 55 to 75 yd (50 to 69 m) |
| Size 3 | Adult Medium | 21" (53 cm) | 8" (20 cm) | 9½" (24 cm) | 65 to 90 yd (59 to 82 m) |
| Size 4 | Adult Large | 22½" (57 cm) | 9" (23 cm) | 10½" (27 cm) | 80 to 110 yd (73 to 101 m) |

*Directions will be shown in the pattern as follows: Size 1 (Size 2, Size 3, Size 4)*

## HAT POWER 2.5
### 2½ STITCHES = 1 INCH (2.5 CM)

### CAST ON STITCHES AND BEGIN KNITTING
Cast on 44 (48, 52, 56) stitches. Choose an edge style. Use the larger needle if you plan to make a roll brim hat in stockinette stitch (knit every stitch). Use the smaller needle if you plan to make the bottom edge in ribbing or garter stitch. Place BOR marker and join in the round being careful not to twist (see page 20).

### RIBBED EDGE
**Round 1:** *K2, p2*; repeat from * to * to end of round.

Repeat round 1 until ribbing is desired length from cast-on edge. Change to larger needle and continue in stockinette stitch (knit every stitch).

### GARTER STITCH EDGE
**Round 1:** Knit.
**Round 2:** Purl.

Repeat rounds 1 and 2 until the garter stitch section is desired length from cast-on edge. Change to larger needle and continue in stockinette stitch (knit every stitch).

### ROLL-BRIM
Use the larger circular needle and begin knitting in stockinette stitch (knit every stitch) immediately.

### HAT BODY
Continue working in stockinette stitch until the length from the cast-on row is:
- 4¼" (4¾", 5¼", 6") [11 (12, 13.5, 15) cm] for short hat
- 5¼" (6", 6¾", 7½") [13.5 (15, 17, 19) cm] for tall hat
- For a roll-brim add 1½" to 2" (4 to 5 cm) extra to the desired length above (unroll edge to measure accurately).

## GAUGE

10 sts and 14 rows = 4" (10 cm) in stockinette stitch

## YARN

Super bulky weight yarn; the approximate yardage for each size is shown in the chart at left.

## NEEDLES AND NOTIONS

US size 15 (10 mm) 16" (41 cm) circular needle or size required to achieve gauge

US size 11 (8 mm) 16" (41 cm) circular needle (or two sizes smaller than size used to achieve gauge) to make an edge of ribbing or garter stitch

US size 15 (10 mm) double-pointed needles or size required to achieve gauge

Optional Magic Loop: above needle sizes in a circular needle at least 40" (101 cm) long

Circular stitch marker

Yarn needle for weaving in ends

## SHAPE TOP

Work decreases to shape the crown of the hat. Notice that the larger sizes require more rows to decrease their greater number of stitches. If you are making one of the smaller sizes then skip the rows that don't apply to your hat size. Change to DPNs when the stitches will no longer fit comfortably around the circular needle.

**Round 1 for size 4 only:**
[Knit 26, k2tog] twice, 54 sts remain.
**Round 2 for size 4 only:** *Knit 7, k2tog*; repeat from * to * to end of round—48 sts remain.
**Round 3 for size 4 only:** Knit.
**Round 3 for size 3 only:**
*K11, k2tog*; repeat from * to * to end of round—48 sts remain.
**Round 4 for sizes 2, 3, and 4 only:**
*Knit 6, k2tog*; repeat from * to * to end of round—42 sts remain.
**Round 5 for sizes 2, 3, and 4 only:** Knit.
**Round 5 for size 1 only:**
[Knit 20, k2tog] twice—42 sts remain.

From this point, all four sizes are worked identically:
**Round 6:** *Knit 5, k2tog*; repeat from * to * to end of round—36 sts remain.
**Round 7:** Knit.
**Round 8:** *Knit 4, k2tog*; repeat from * to * to end of round—30 sts remain.
**Round 9:** *Knit 3, k2tog*; repeat from * to * to end of round—24 sts remain.
**Round 10:** *Knit 2, k2tog*; repeat from * to * to end of round—18 sts remain.
**Round 11:** *Knit 1, k2tog*; repeat from * to * to end of round—12 sts remain.
**Round 12:** *K2tog*; repeat from * to * to end of round—6 sts remain.

To finish the hat, cut the yarn leaving a tail at least 8" (20 cm) long. Using a yarn needle, thread the tail through the remaining stitches and pass through the hole in the top of the hat to the inside. Pull the tail firmly to close the hole and weave the ends into the stitches on the inside of the hat to secure.

# Hat Gallery

Now that you've learned the basics of making a hat you'll be able to experiment with different yarns. I had a wonderful time raiding the shelves in my yarn shop to come up with different yarn combinations and textures. All of these examples follow the simple patterns in the Hat Power section.

## SILK AND CASHMERE

This hat feels as luxurious as it sounds. A strand of cashmere was combined with a strand of hand painted silk. It is soft and has a beautiful drape. The hat was designed for an adult friend who is a very tiny person (with a big personality).

**Pattern:** 5½ stitches = 1 inch (2.5 cm)

**Variations:** The edge was knit with k4, p4 ribbing instead of k2, p2 ribbing.

**Size:** The size shown is Size 2, 19" (48.3 cm) finished hat circumference. Shaping for the crown was started when the length from the cast on edge was 6½" (16.5 cm). The finished hat height is 9½" (24.1 cm).

**Yarn A:** Super fine weight brushed yarn, 155 yd (142 m)

**Shown:** Filatura di Crosa *Superior*; 70% cashmere, 30% silk; 328 yd (300 m)/0.875 oz (25g); color #30 Orchid, 1 ball (A fine mohair can be substituted for yarn A.)

**Yarn B:** Super fine weight smooth yarn, 155 yd (142 m)

**Shown:** Hand Maiden *Sea Silk*; 70% silk, 30% Seacell; 437 yd (400 m)/3.5 oz (100 g); color Morgana, 1 skein

# THICK AND THIN

I was surprised by how beautiful this hat was after the knitting was finished. Often we knit thick and thin yarns at a loose tension for scarves. This hat was knit at a tension a bit tighter than suggested by the yarn label. The result seems like an Impressionist painting, the colors are enhanced by the ebb and flow of the texture. The fiber content of the yarn gives the stitches a soft feel and lovely drape.

**Pattern:** 5 stitches = 1 inch (2.5 cm)

**Size:** The size shown is Size 2, 19" (48.3 cm) finished hat circumference. Shaping for the crown was started when the length from the cast on edge was 5½" (14 cm). The finished hat height is 8" (20.3 cm).

**Yarn:** Medium weight thick and thin yarn, 120 yd (110 m)

**Shown:** Misti Alpaca *Baby Me Boo*; 50% baby alpaca, 30% merino, 20% bamboo; 174 yd (159 m)/3.5 oz (100 g); color Lila's Palace, 1 skein

# BULKY WATCH CAP

I love the look of a watch cap, especially on guys. This is a basic chunky weight wool yarn that is made much more interesting with its tweed accents. For a trendy look, the rib section can be unfolded so the hat can be worn as a slouch hat instead. For a watch cap, decide how much height you want for the ribbing and then knit twice that length of ribbing. For a slouch hat ask your teenager since we all know how dangerous it is to make something without their approval!

**Pattern:** 3.5 sts = 1" (2.5 cm)

**Variations:** The k2, p2 ribbing section is knit for 5" (12.5 cm) before changing to stockinette stitch (all knit).

**Size:** The hat shown is size 3, 20½" (52 cm) finished hat circumference. Shaping for the crown was started when the length from the cast-on edge was 8" (20 cm). The finished hat height is 11" (28 cm) with the ribbing unfolded and 8½" (21.5 cm) with the ribbing folded in half.

**Yarn:** Bulky weight smooth tweed yarn, 123 yd (112 m)

**Shown:** Cascade Yarns *128 Tweed*, 90% wool, 9% acrylic, 1% nylon; 128 yd (117 m) per 3.5 oz (100g) skein, color #7701, 1 skein.

# INSTANT SUCCESS

If you want to finish a hat in the time it takes to watch a movie, then grab your big needles and some super bulky yarn. To keep the hat from being too heavy, choose a yarn that is loosely spun and airy like this hand-dyed merino. Also, hats made from really heavy yarns should be kept on the shorter side. Set aside any rigid expectations when working with these charming, artisan, hand-dyed yarns—the colors can be quirky. Instead of being dismayed by color differences between two balls, make the best of it and create a stripe!

**Pattern:** 2.5 sts = 1" (2.5 cm)

**Variations:** The hat has a four-row stripe of contrast color used for the ribbing and again right before the shaping.

**Size:** The hat shown is size 3, 20½" (52 cm) finished hat circumference. Shaping for the crown was started when the length from the cast-on edge was 5½" (14 cm). The finished hat height is 8" (20 cm).

**Yarn:** Super bulky weight single ply yarn. 70 yd (64 m) total: 46 yd (42 m) pink, 24 yd (22 m) green.

**Shown:** Malabrigo *Rasta*, 100% merino wool; 89 yd (81 m) per 5.25 oz (150 g) skein, 1 skein. Color: Arco Iris, two differently shaded skeins if color contrast is desired.

For mitten directions see Mitten Power 2.5, page 55.

# Mittens

## Mitten Basics

Mittens may seem a bit daunting to make because of their shape, but once you follow the step-by-step directions you'll be amazed by how simple it is to make a pair. The most complicated part is casting on to double-pointed needles but after that it's smooth sailing. As with the instructions for the basic hat, you will be making this pair out of worsted weight wool.

## STEP-BY-STEP- GUIDE FOR KNITTING MITTENS

*This step-by-step guide is intended for the knitter who has never made a pair of mittens. Knitting directions are written in plain text, followed by further explanation in italics.*

Human hands have much more variation in size than heads so you'll find a lot more sizes to choose from. When working from a pattern with a large number of sizes, it's a good idea to photocopy the pattern before you start so you can highlight all the directions applying to the size you are making.

### GAUGE

20 sts = 4" (10 cm) in stockinette stitch

**Important:** Make a gauge swatch before you start knitting. It's the only way to make sure the mittens will turn out the way you expect (see page 10).

### YARN

Medium weight yarn; approximate yardage for each size is shown in chart.

Shown: Cascade Yarns *220 Wool*, 100% wool; 220 yd (201 m) per 3.5 oz (100 g) skein

### NEEDLES AND NOTIONS

US size 7 (4.5 mm) double-pointed needles or size required to achieve gauge

US size 5 (3.75 mm) double-pointed needles (or two sizes smaller than size used to achieve gauge)

Optional Magic Loop: above needle sizes in a circular needle at least 32" (81 cm) long.

Circular stitch markers

Small stitch holder (or waste yarn)

Yarn needle for weaving in ends

### MITTEN BASICS: Size, Finished Dimensions, and Yardage

|        | To Fit Size | Finished Hand Circumference | Finished Length | Approximate Yardage |
|--------|-------------|------------------------------|-----------------|---------------------|
| Size 1 | 2 to 4 year | 5½" (14 cm) | 5¾" (15 cm) | 60 yd (55 m) |
| Size 2 | 5 to 7 year | 6¼" (16 cm) | 7" (18 cm) | 80 yd (73 m) |
| Size 3 | 8 to 10 year | 6¾" (17 cm) | 7¾" (20 cm) | 100 yd (91 m) |
| Size 4 | 12 year to Women's Small | 7¼" (18 cm) | 8½" (22 cm) | 110 yd (101 m) |
| Size 5 | Women's Medium | 7½" (19 cm) | 9" (23 cm) | 130 yd (119 m) |
| Size 6 | Women's Large/Men's Small | 8" (20 cm) | 9¾" (25 cm) | 150 yd (137 m) |
| Size 7 | Men's Medium | 8½" (22 cm) | 10½" (27 cm) | 175 yd (160 m) |
| Size 8 | Men's Large | 9" (23 cm) | 11½" (29 cm) | 195 yd (173 m) |

*Directions will be shown in the pattern as follows: Size 1 (Size 2, Size 3, Size 4) (Size 5, Size 6, Size 7, Size 8)*

## CAST ON STITCHES
## AND BEGIN KNITTING CUFF

Make both mittens alike.

Using smaller needles, cast on 28 (32, 32, 36) (36, 40, 40, 44) sts. Place BOR marker and join in the round being careful not to twist.

*Double-pointed needles generally come in sets of five. The stitches can be divided between three or four needles; the extra free needle is used to knit. If you are using three needles then a triangle will be formed; four needles form a square. Cast on all the required stitches for the size you are making to one needle and then transfer them, evenly divided, to the other two or three needles (1).*

2

3

*Keeping the needles in this arrangement, pick them up and use the free needle to begin knitting into the first cast-on stitch on the left needle using the working yarn from the last stitch on the right needle (4). Knit all of the stitches from the left needle on to the free needle. When the left needle is empty it becomes the new free needle and is used to knit the stitches on the next needle and so on. Note that you will begin the k2, p2 pattern on the very first row.*

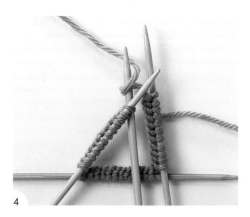
1

*As with knitting a hat in the round, it is important that the stitches not be twisted when joining to knit mittens in the round. Lay the needles down on a table in a triangle (2) or square (3) making sure that the bump at the bottom of the stitches is lined up facing the center of the triangle (or square). The first stitch that was cast on is on the left needle and the last stitch, connected to the working yarn, is on the right needle.*

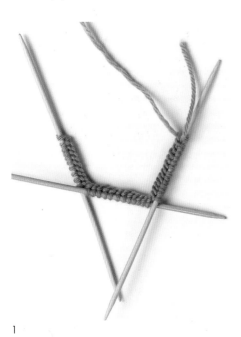
4

**Round 1:** *K2, p2*; repeat from * to * to end of round.

Repeat round 1 until cuff measures 1½" (2", 2¼", 2½") (2½", 2¾", 2¾", 3") [4 (5, 6, 6.5) (6.5, 7, 7, 7.5) cm].

*The best way to deal with the extra needles holding stitches waiting to be worked is to ignore them! Focus on the two needles being used at any given time and hold them to the front while the other needles stay out of the way to the sides and back (5). If you find that the needles are falling out of the stitches while you work then change to longer double-pointed needles or bamboo needles if you are using metal ones.*

*Once you have knit an entire round place a marker to indicate the beginning of the round. You may find it easier to keep the BOR marker in its place if you readjust the stitches so that the marker falls in the middle of a needle.*

## THUMB GUSSET

*In preparation to make the thumb gusset some adjustments will be made to the stitch count. Also note that you will be changing to the larger needles since the ribbing section is now finished.*

Change to larger needles.

**Round 1:** Knit.

**Round 2 for sizes 1, 2, 3, and 4:** Inc 1, knit to end of round.

**Round 2 for sizes 5, 6, 7, and 8:** Knit.

**Round 3 for sizes 5, 6, 7, and 8 only:** Inc 1, knit to end of round. Skip for other sizes.

**There should be:**
29 (33, 33, 37) (37, 41, 41, 45) sts.

*The thumb gusset is a triangular-shaped addition that is formed by increasing stitches on one side of the mitten. The increases are started a few rounds after the cuff is completed. The thumb gusset will wrap around the angled portion of the thumb and provide the base to which the thumb stitches are attached to form a tube (6). Markers are used to delineate the*

(continued)

5

6

*beginning and end of the gusset section. You'll find it easier to use the same color markers for the gusset but make sure their color contrasts to the color used for the BOR marker. I find it easiest to put all the gusset stitches on one needle (see illustration #6, page 41). Once the markers are set it's easy to get into a rhythm of knitting increase rows followed by plain knit rows. Depending on the size you are making some of the rows will be skipped, so pay attention to the specific directions for the size you are making. Also, the larger sizes require more rows, so pay attention to the direction to proceed ahead for the smaller sizes.*

**Round 4:** Knit 14 (16, 16, 18) (18, 20, 20, 22) sts, pm, k1, pm, k to end of round.

**Round 5:** Knit to first marker, sm, M1L, k1, M1R, sm, k to end of round—3 sts between gusset markers.

**Round 6:** Knit to end of round, slipping markers as you come to them.

**Round 7 for size 1 and 4 only:** Knit to end of round, slipping markers as you come to them. Skip for other sizes.

**Round 8:** Knit to first marker, sm, M1L, knit to next marker, M1R, sm, k to end of round—5 sts between markers.

**Round 9:** Knit to end of round, slipping markers as you come to them.

**Round 10 for size 1 and 4 only:** Knit to end of round, slipping markers as you come to them. Skip for other sizes.

**Round 11:** Knit to first marker, sm, M1L, knit to next marker, M1R, sm, k to end of round—7 sts between markers.

**Round 12:** Knit to end of round, slipping markers as you come to them.

**Round 13 for sizes 1, 2, 3, 4, and 6 only:** Knit to end of round, slipping markers as you come to them. Skip for other sizes.

**Round 14:** Knit to first marker, sm, M1L, knit to next marker, M1R, sm, k to end of round—9 sts between markers.

**Round 15:** Knit to end of round, slipping markers as you come to them.

**Size 1: Proceed to round 29.**

**Round 16 for sizes 2, 3, 4, 5, and 6 only:** Knit to end of round, slipping markers as you come to them. Skip for other sizes.

**Round 17 for sizes 2, 3, 4, 5, 6, 7, and 8 only:** Knit to first marker, sm, M1L, knit to next marker, M1R, sm, k to end of round—11 sts between markers.

**Round 18 for sizes 2, 3, 4, 5, 6, 7, and 8 only:** Knit to end of round, slipping markers as you come to them.

**Round 19 for size 2, 3, 4, 5, 6, and 8 only:** Knit to end of round, slipping markers as you come to them. Skip for other sizes.

**Sizes 2, 3, and 4: Proceed to round 29.**

**Round 20 for sizes 5, 6, 7, and 8 only:** Knit to first marker, sm, M1L, knit to next marker, M1R, sm, k to end of round—13 sts between markers.

**Rounds 21–22 for sizes 5, 6, 7, and 8 only:** Knit to end of round, slipping markers as you come to them.

**Size 5: Proceed to round 29.**

**Round 23 for sizes 6, 7, and 8 only:** Knit to first marker, sm, M1L, knit to next marker, M1R, sm, k to end of round—15 sts between markers.

**Rounds 24–25 for sizes 6, 7, and 8 only:** Knit to end of round, slipping markers as you come to them.

**Size 6: Proceed to round 29.**

**Round 26 for sizes 7 and 8 only:** Knit to first marker, sm, M1L, knit to next marker, M1R, sm, k to end of round—17 sts between markers.

**Rounds 27–28 for sizes 7 and 8 only:** Knit to end of round, slipping markers as you come to them.

**Round 29, all sizes:** Transfer gusset stitches to holder as follows: Knit to marker, remove marker, place next 9 (11, 11, 11) (13, 15, 17, 17) sts on holder, remove marker, use backward thumb loop to cast on 1 (1, 2, 1,) (2, 1, 2, 1) st over gap left by gusset stitches, k to end of round.

*Once all the gusset stitches have been completed, then a final round is worked to transfer the gusset stitches to a holder and one or more stitches is cast on to bridge the gap that is left once the stitches have been removed. You can use a small stitch holder for the gusset stitches but I prefer to use a short length (about 8" [20 cm]) of contrast yarn threaded on a yarn needle (7).*

7

To make a backward thumb loop, see the directions on page 13.

The gusset sts will remain on their holder until the shaping is finished for the mitten tip (8).

8

**Round 30:** Knit.
**Round 31 for size 1:** K14, k2tog, k13.
**Round 31 for size 2:** K16, k2tog, k15.
**Round 31 for size 4:** K18, k2tog, k17.
**Round 31 for size 6:** K19, k2tog, k18.
Skip round 31 for sizes 3, 5, 7 and 8.
**There should be:**
28 (32, 34, 36) (38, 40, 42, 45) sts.
**Round 32:** Knit.

Repeat round 32 until length from cuff is approximately 3" (3½", 4", 4½") (5", 5½", 6", 6½") [7.5 (9, 10, 11.5) (12.5, 14, 15, 16.5) cm]. At this point, the total length from cast-on row should be 4½" (5½", 6¼", 7") (7½", 8¼", 8¾", 9½") [11.5 (14, 16, 18) (19, 21, 22, 24) cm].

**SHAPE TIP OF MITTEN**
*Once the desired length has been completed it is time to work some decreases to taper the tip of the mitten. The shaping starts out slowly with plain knit rows between decrease rows at the beginning but the last few rows eliminate the plain knit rows between decrease rows so that the tip is more sharply tapered. Depending on the size you are making some of the rows will be skipped, so pay attention to the specific directions for the size you are making. Also, the larger sizes require more rows, so pay attention to the direction to proceed ahead for the smaller sizes.*
**Round 1 for size 1, 2, 4, and 6 only:** Knit.
**Round 1 for size 3:** [Knit 15, k2tog] twice—32 sts remain.
**Round 1 for size 5:** [Knit 17, k2tog] twice—36 sts remain.
**Round 1 for size 7:** [Knit 19, k2tog] twice—40 sts remain.
**Round 1 for size 8:** Knit 22, k2tog, knit to end of round—44 sts remain.
**Round 2:** *Knit 5 (6, 6, 7) (7, 8, 8, 9) sts, k2tog*; repeat from * to * to end of round—24 (28, 28, 32) (32, 36, 36, 40) sts remain.
**Round 3:** Knit.

(continued)

**Round 4:** *Knit 4 (5, 5, 6) (6, 7, 7, 8) sts, k2tog*; repeat from * to * to end of round—20 (24, 24, 28) (28, 32, 32, 36) sts remain.

**Round 5:** Knit.

**Round 6:** *Knit 3 (4, 4, 5) (5, 6, 6, 7) sts, k2tog*; repeat from * to * to end of round—16 (20, 20, 24) (24, 28, 28, 32) sts remain.

**Round 7:** Knit.

**Round 8:** *Knit 2 (3, 3, 4) (4, 5, 5, 6) sts, k2tog*; repeat from * to * to end of round—12 (16, 16, 20) (20, 24, 24, 28) sts remain.

**Round 9 for sizes 6, 7, and 8 only:** Knit. Skip for other sizes.

**Round 10:** *Knit 1 (2, 2, 3) (3, 4, 4, 5) sts, k2tog*; repeat from * to * to end of round—8 (12, 12, 16) (16, 20, 20, 24) sts remain.

**Size 1: Proceed to round 15.**

**Round 11 for sizes 2, 3, 4, 5, 6, 7, and 8 only:** *Knit - (1, 1, 2) (2, 3, 3, 4) sts, k2tog*; repeat from * to * to end of round— - (8, 8, 12) (12, 16, 16, 20) sts remain.

**Sizes 2 and 3: Proceed to round 15.**

**Round 12 for sizes 4, 5, 6, 7, and 8 only:** *Knit - (-, -, 1) (1, 2, 2, 3) sts, k2tog*; repeat from * to * to end of round— - (-, -, 8) (8, 12, 12, 16) sts remain.

**Sizes 4 and 5:** Proceed to directions for finishing main portion of mitten.

**Round 13 for sizes 6, 7, and 8 only:** *Knit - (-, -, -) (-, 1, 1, 2) sts, k2tog*; repeat from * to * to end of round— - (-, -, -) (-, 8, 8, 12) sts remain.

**Size 6 and 7:** Proceed to directions for finishing main portion of mitten.

**Round 14 for size 8 only:** *K1, k2tog*; repeat from * to * to end of round—8 sts remain.

**Size 8:** Proceed to directions for finishing main portion of mitten.

**Round 15 for sizes 1, 2, and 3 only:** *K2tog*; repeat from * to * to end of round—4 sts remain.

## FINISHING MAIN PORTION OF MITTEN

Cut yarn leaving an 8" (20 cm) tail. Thread tail onto yarn needle and draw through remaining stitches on needle. Pull to tighten loop and pass yarn needle to inside of mitten and weave yarn tail through stitches to secure.

*Once the decreases have been accomplished you will need to close the top. Cut the yarn leaving a tail at least 8" (20 cm) long and thread the tail on a yarn needle. Pass the yarn needle through the final stitches (working in the same order as you would if knitting) to form a draw string (9). Pull the tail tightly to close the hole at the top and then pass the needle through the hole to the inside of the mitten. Give the tail an extra tug on the inside and weave it through the stitches on the inside to secure.*

9

## MITTEN THUMB

Remove gusset stitches from stitch holder and distribute on three DPNs.

*Now it's time to attach stitches to the top of the gusset which forms the base for the thumb. Remove the gusset stitches from the holder (or string) and distribute them on double-pointed needles. Begin transferring the stitches to the needles at the right side of the gap (when holding the mitten with the ribbing at the bottom) and put more stitches on the first and second needle than the third (10).*

Attach yarn leaving an 8" (20 cm) tail, use the third needle to pick up and knit 3 (3, 3, 3) (4, 4, 4, 4) stitches over gap. Place marker to indicate beginning of round, join in the round and continue to knit as follows:

*You will find it easier to pick up stitches over the gap if you rotate the mitten so the ribbing is at the top. Start the working yarn by picking up and knitting stitches over the gap as indicated (these stitches will be on your third needle) (11). Be sure to leave a tail at least 8" (20 cm) long. At the end of the first full round, two decreases will be worked to incorporate the picked-up stitches with the existing gusset stitches. Remember that the round begins on needle one or use a BOR marker, if desired.*

**Round 1 for sizes 1 (2, 3, 4):** Knit until 4 sts remain before end of round, ssk, k1, k2tog (you will need to reposition the BOR marker to fall after the k2tog).

**Round 1 for sizes (5, 6, 7, 8):** Knit until 5 sts remain before end of round, ssk, k2, k2tog (you will need to reposition the BOR marker to fall after the k2tog). You should have 10 (12, 12, 12) (15, 17, 19, 19) sts.

**Round 2:** Knit.

(continued)

10

11

12

Repeat round 2 for 5 (7, 9, 9) (11, 12, 14, 14) more rows or until length from beginning of thumb (where stitches were picked up over gusset space) equals ¾" (1", 1¼", 1¼") (1½", 1¾", 2", 2") [2 (2.5, 3, 3) (4, 4.5, 5, 5) cm].

*Once the thumb stitches are established you'll find that the knitting progresses very quickly (12).*

## SHAPE TIP OF THUMB
Work decreases to taper tip of thumb.

*The decreases to shape the tip of the mitten thumb and the closing of the hole are completed in much the same way as the mitten tip, only in miniature.*

**Round 1 for sizes 1, 7, and 8:** K2tog, knit to end of round.

**Round 1 for size 6:** K2tog, k6, k2tog, k to end of round.

**Round 1 for all other sizes:** Knit.
**There should be:**
9 (12, 12, 12) (15, 15, 18, 18) sts.

**Round 2:** *K1 (2, 2, 2) (3, 3, 4, 4), k2tog*; repeat from * to * to end of round— 6 (9, 9, 9) (12, 12, 15, 15) sts remain.

**Round 3:** Knit.

**Round 4 for size 1:** *K1, k2tog*; repeat from * to * to end of round—4 sts remain.

**Round 4 for size 2, 3, 4, 5, 6, 7, and 8 only:** *K - (1, 1, 2) (2, 2, 3, 3), k2tog*; repeat from * to * to end of round— - (6, 6, 6) (9, 9, 12, 12) sts remain.

**Sizes 1, 2, 3, and 4:** Proceed to directions for finishing thumb.

**Round 5 for sizes 5, 6, 7, and 8 only:** *K – (-, -, -) (1, 1, 2, 2), k2tog*; repeat from * to * to end of round— - (-, -, -) (6, 6, 9, 9) sts remain.

**Sizes 5 and 6:** Proceed to directions for finishing thumb.

**Round 6 for sizes 7 and 8 only:** *K1, k2tog*; repeat from * to * to end of round—6 sts remain.

## FINISHING THUMB
Remove marker and cut yarn leaving a tail at least 8" (20 cm) long. Thread tail onto yarn needle and draw through remaining stitches on needle. Pull to tighten loop and pass to inside of thumb and weave through stitches to secure. Using yarn tail at the base of the thumb, close any gaps that might remain and secure by weaving through stitches.

Repeat directions for second mitten. To finish mittens weave in all ends and steam lightly.

# Mitten Extras

There aren't as many ways to change the essential look of a mitten as you can with a hat, but you can still express your creativity with how you get started with the cuff.

## CHANGING THE CUFF

In the Mitten Power chapter most of the mittens begin with a k2, p2 ribbing. One easy way to get a different look is to make the ribbing section twice as long. Fold it back as a cuff or keep it long and tucked up your sleeve. You can also change the look of the cuff by using different stitches. The simple striped hat (page 84) has a mini cable worked into the rib. You can use this design in place of any k2, p2 ribbing.

Instead of ribbing, make the cuff in garter stitch or seed stitch. To make garter stitch in the round, alternate one round of knit with one round of purl. Seed stitch is made on an even number of stitches by working the first round as k1, p1 and the second round as p1, k1; repeat rounds 1 and 2 until the cuff is the desired length. My friend Karen, the superb technical editor of this book, had another cute idea. Start the mitten with a rolled edge like a hat. After a few rows of all knit stitch, work two or three rows of ribbing to stop the roll and then change back to stockinette stitch (all knit).

## CUSTOM FIT

Making a hat that fits is quite simple because human heads don't have a lot of variance in size or shape. The same does not hold true for our hands. There's a big difference between a child's hand and an adult's hand and there's a lot of variance in shape. Once you learn the basic mitten pattern you can explore some creative possibilities by modifying the pattern to fit exactly the way you want. For instance, if you have exceptionally long fingers then add some extra rows to the mitten before the tip is shaped. Nothing is more annoying than a gusset that doesn't fit so add or subtract plain knit rows to the gusset shaping to make it longer or shorter. The same applies to the thumb— add a few rows for extra length or pick up and knit a few more stitches on the first thumb row for extra circumference.

## MITTEN CORD

Nothing makes a pair of kid's mittens more special that a mitten cord! You can make a crochet chain or knit an I-cord (page 65). Or keep it really simple by casting on enough stitches for the desired length, knit one row, and then bind off. To get the right length, measure from the center back to the wrist with the arm slightly bent and double the length. If desired, you can add a few extra inches for growing room and make a knot in the center of the cord.

# Mitten Power

This is the same pattern as the one used in the Mitten Basics section but without the longer explanations. I encourage you to use high-quality, smooth wool until you become comfortable with making basic mittens. All of the mittens in this section have a ribbed cuff but you could certainly substitute a cuff of garter stitch instead.

### MITTEN POWER 5.0: Size, Finished Dimensions, and Yardage

| | To Fit Size | Finished Hand Circumference | Finished Length | Approximate Yardage |
|---|---|---|---|---|
| Size 1 | 2 to 4 year | 5½" (14 cm) | 5¾" (15 cm) | 60 yd (55 m) |
| Size 2 | 5 to 7 year | 6¼" (16 cm) | 7" (18 cm) | 80 yd (73 m) |
| Size 3 | 8 to 10 year | 6¾" (17 cm) | 7¾" (20 cm) | 100 yd (91 m) |
| Size 4 | 12 year to Women's Small | 7¼" (18 cm) | 8½" (22 cm) | 110 yd (101 m) |
| Size 5 | Women's Medium | 7½" (19 cm) | 9" (23 cm) | 130 yd (119 m) |
| Size 6 | Women's Large/ Men's Small | 8" (20 cm) | 9¾" (25 cm) | 150 yd (137 m) |
| Size 7 | Men's Medium | 8½" (22 cm) | 10½" (27 cm) | 175 yd (160 m) |
| Size 8 | Men's Large | 9" (23 cm) | 11½" (29 cm) | 195 yd (173 m) |

*Directions will be shown in the pattern as follows: Size 1 (Size 2, Size 3, Size 4) (Size 5, Size 6, Size 7, Size 8)*

## MITTEN POWER 5.0
### 5 STITCHES = 1 INCH (2.5 CM)

**CAST ON STITCHES
AND BEGIN KNITTING CUFF**
Make both mittens alike.
Using smaller needles, cast on 28 (32, 32, 36) (36, 40, 40, 44) sts. Place BOR marker and join in the round being careful not to twist (see page 20).
**Round 1:** *K2, p2*; repeat from * to * to end of round.
Repeat round 1 until cuff measures 1½" (2", 2¼", 2½") (2½", 2¾", 2¾", 3") [4 (5, 6, 6.5) (6.5, 7, 7, 7.5) cm].

**THUMB GUSSET**
Change to larger needles.
**Round 1:** Knit.
**Round 2 for sizes 1, 2, 3, and 4:** Inc 1, knit to end of round.
**Round 2 for sizes 5, 6, 7, and 8:** Knit.
**Round 3 for sizes 5, 6, 7, and 8 only:** Inc 1, knit to end of round. Skip for other sizes.
**There should be:**
29, (33, 33, 37) (37, 41, 41, 45) sts.
**Round 4:** Knit 14 (16, 16, 18) (18, 20, 20, 22) sts, pm, k1, pm, k to end of round.

**Round 5:** Knit to first marker, sm, M1L, k1, M1R, sm, k to end of round—3 sts between gusset markers.

**Round 6:** Knit to end of round, slipping markers as you come to them.

**Round 7 for size 1 and 4 only:** Knit to end of round, slipping markers as you come to them. Skip for other sizes.

**Round 8:** Knit to first marker, sm, M1L, knit to next marker, M1R, sm, k to end of round—5 sts between markers.

**Round 9:** Repeat round 6.

**Round 10 for size 1 and 4 only:** Repeat round 6. Skip for other sizes.

**Round 11:** Knit to first marker, sm, M1L, knit to next marker, M1R, sm, k to end of round—7 sts between markers.

**Round 12:** Repeat round 6.

**Round 13 for sizes 1, 2, 3, 4, and 6 only:** Repeat round 6. Skip for other sizes.

**Round 14:** Knit to first marker, sm, M1L, knit to next marker, M1R, sm, k to end of round—9 sts between markers.

**Round 15:** Repeat round 6.

**Size 1: Proceed to round 29.**

**Round 16 for sizes 2, 3, 4, 5, and 6 only:** Repeat round 6. Skip for other sizes.

**Round 17 for sizes 2, 3, 4, 5, 6, 7, and 8 only:** Knit to first marker, sm, M1L, knit to next marker, M1R, sm, k to end of round—11 sts between markers.

**Round 18 for sizes 2, 3, 4, 5, 6, 7, and 8 only:** Repeat round 6.

**Round 19 for size 2, 3, 4, 5, 6, and 8 only:** Repeat round 6. Skip for other sizes.

**Sizes 2, 3, and 4: Proceed to round 29.**

**Round 20 for sizes 5, 6, 7, and 8 only:** Knit to first marker, sm, M1L, knit to next marker, M1R, sm, k to end of round—13 sts between markers.

**Rounds 21–22 for sizes 5, 6, 7, and 8 only:** Repeat round 6.

**Size 5: Proceed to round 29.**

**Round 23 for sizes 6, 7, and 8 only:** Knit to first marker, sm, M1L, knit to next marker, M1R, sm, k to end of round—15 sts between markers.

**Rounds 24–25 for sizes 6, 7, and 8 only:** Repeat round 6.

**Size 6: Proceed to round 29.**

**Round 26 for sizes 7 and 8 only:** Knit to first marker, sm, M1L, knit to next marker, M1R, sm, k to end of round—17 sts between markers.

**Rounds 27–28 for sizes 7 and 8 only:** Repeat round 6.

**Round 29, all sizes:** Knit to marker, remove marker, place next 9 (11, 11, 11) (13, 15, 17, 17) sts on holder, remove marker, use backward thumb loop to cast on 1 (1, 2, 1,) (2, 1, 2, 1) st over gap left by gusset stitches, k to end of round.

**Round 30:** Knit.

**Round 31 for size 1:** K14, k2tog, k13.

**Round 31 for size 2:** K16, k2tog, k15.

**Round 31 for size 4:** K18, k2tog, k17.

**Round 31 for size 6:** K19, k2tog, k18.

Skip round 31 for sizes 3, 5, 7 and 8.

**There should be:**

28 (32, 34, 36) (38, 40, 42, 45) sts.

(continued)

**Round 32:** Knit.

Repeat round 32 until length from cuff is approximately 3" (3½", 4", 4½") (5", 5½", 6", 6½") [7.5 (9, 10, 11.5) (12.5, 14, 15, 16.5) cm]. At this point, the total length from cast-on row should be 4½" (5½", 6¼", 7") (7½", 8¼", 8¾", 9½") [11.5 (14, 16, 18) (19, 21, 22, 24) cm].

**SHAPE TIP OF MITTEN**

Work decreases to shape the tip of the mitten.

**Round 1 for size 1, 2, 4, and 6 only:** Knit.

**Round 1 for size 3:** [Knit 15, k2tog] twice—32 sts remain.

**Round 1 for size 5:** [Knit 17, k2tog] twice—36 sts remain.

**Round 1 for size 7:** [Knit 19, k2tog] twice—40 sts remain.

**Round 1 for size 8:** Knit 22, k2tog, knit to end of round—44 sts remain.

**Round 2:** *Knit 5 (6, 6, 7) (7, 8, 8, 9) sts, k2tog*; repeat from * to * to end of round—24 (28, 28, 32) (32, 36, 36, 40) sts remain.

**Round 3:** Knit.

**Round 4:** *Knit 4 (5, 5, 6) (6, 7, 7, 8) sts, k2tog*; repeat from * to * to end of round—20 (24, 24, 28) (28, 32, 32, 36) sts remain.

**Round 5:** Knit.

**Round 6:** *Knit 3 (4, 4, 5) (5, 6, 6, 7) sts, k2tog*; repeat from * to * to end of round—16 (20, 20, 24) (24, 28, 28, 32) sts remain.

**Round 7:** Knit.

**Round 8:** *Knit 2 (3, 3, 4) (4, 5, 5, 6) sts, k2tog*; repeat from * to * to end of round—12 (16, 16, 20) (20, 24, 24, 28) sts remain.

**Round 9 for sizes 6, 7, and 8 only:** Knit. Skip for other sizes.

**Round 10:** *Knit 1 (2, 2, 3) (3, 4, 4, 5) sts, k2tog*; repeat from * to * to end of round—8 (12, 12, 16) (16, 20, 20, 24) sts remain.

**Size 1: Proceed to round 15.**

**Round 11 for sizes 2, 3, 4, 5, 6, 7, and 8 only:** *Knit - (1, 1, 2) (2, 3, 3, 4) sts, k2tog*; repeat from * to * to end of round— - (8, 8, 12) (12, 16, 16, 20) sts remain.

**Sizes 2 and 3: Proceed to round 15.**

**Round 12 for sizes 4, 5, 6, 7, and 8 only:** *Knit - (-, -, 1) (1, 2, 2, 3) sts, k2tog*; repeat from * to * to end of round— - (-, -, 8) (8, 12, 12, 16) sts remain.

**Sizes 4 and 5:** Proceed to directions for finishing main portion of mitten.

**Round 13 for sizes 6, 7, and 8 only:** *Knit - (-, -, -) (-, 1, 1, 2) sts, k2tog*; repeat from * to * to end of round— - (-, -, -) (-, 8, 8, 12) sts remain.

**Size 6 and 7:** Proceed to directions for finishing main portion of mitten.

**Round 14 for size 8 only:** *K1, k2tog*; repeat from * to * to end of round— 8 sts remain.

**Size 8:** Proceed to directions for finishing main portion of mitten.

**Round 15 for sizes 1, 2, and 3 only:** *K2tog*; repeat from * to * to end of round—4 sts remain.

**FINISHING MAIN PORTION OF MITTEN**

Cut yarn leaving an 8" (20 cm) tail. Thread tail onto yarn needle and draw through remaining stitches on needle. Pull to tighten loop and pass yarn needle to inside of mitten and weave yarn tail through stitches to secure.

**MITTEN THUMB**

Remove gusset stitches from stitch holder and distribute on three DPNs. Attach yarn leaving an 8" (20 cm) tail, pick up and knit 3 (3, 3, 3) (4, 4, 4, 4) stitches over gap. Place marker to indicate beginning of round, join in the round and continue to knit as follows:

**Round 1 for sizes 1 (2, 3, 4):** Knit until 4 sts remain before end of round, ssk, k1, k2tog (you will need to reposition the BOR marker to fall after the k2tog).

**Round 1 for sizes (5, 6, 7, 8):** Knit until 5 sts remain before end of round, ssk, k2, k2tog (you will need to reposition the BOR marker to fall after the k2tog).
**You should have:**
10 (12, 12, 12) (15, 17, 19, 19) sts.
**Round 2:** Knit.
   Repeat round 2 for 5 (7, 9, 9) (11, 12, 14, 14) more rows or until length from beginning of thumb (where stitches were picked up over gusset space) equals ¾" (1", 1¼", 1¼") (1½", 1¾", 2", 2") [2 (2.5, 3, 3) (4, 4.5, 5, 5) cm].

## SHAPE TIP OF THUMB
Work decreases to taper tip of thumb.
**Round 1 for sizes 1, 7, and 8:** K2tog, knit to end of round.
**Round 1 for size 6:** K2tog, k6, k2tog, k to end of round.
**Round 1 for all other sizes:** Knit.
**There should be:**
9 (12, 12, 12) (15, 15, 18, 18) sts.
**Round 2:** *K1 (2, 2, 2) (3, 3, 4, 4), k2tog*; repeat from * to * to end of round—
6 (9, 9, 9) (12, 12, 15, 15) sts remain.
**Round 3:** Knit.
**Round 4 for size 1:** *K1, k2tog*; repeat from * to * to end of round—4 sts remain.

**Round 4 for size 2, 3, 4, 5, 6, 7, and 8 only:** *K - (1, 1, 2) (2, 2, 3, 3), k2tog*; repeat from * to * to end of round—
- (6, 6, 6) (9, 9, 12, 12) sts remain.
**Sizes 1, 2, 3, and 4:** Proceed to directions for finishing thumb.
**Round 5 for sizes 5, 6, 7, and 8 only:** *K – (-, -, -) (1, 1, 2, 2), k2tog*; repeat from * to * to end of round—
- (-, -, -) (6, 6, 9, 9) sts remain.
**Sizes 5 and 6:** Proceed to directions for finishing thumb.
**Round 6 for sizes 7 and 8 only:** *K1, k2tog*; repeat from * to * to end of round—6 sts remain.

## FINISHING THUMB
Cut yarn leaving a tail at least 8" (20 cm) long. Thread tail onto yarn needle and draw through remaining stitches on needle. Pull to tighten loop and pass to inside of thumb and weave through stitches to secure. Using yarn tail at the base of the thumb, close any gaps that might remain and secure by weaving through stitches.

   Repeat directions for second mitten. To finish mittens weave in all ends and steam lightly.

## MITTEN POWER 3.5: Size, Finished Dimensions, and Yardage

|  | To Fit Size | Finished Hand Circumference | Finished Length | Approximate Yardage |
|---|---|---|---|---|
| **Size 1** | 7 to 10 year | 6½" (17 cm) | 7¾" (20 cm) | 75 yd (69 m) |
| **Size 2** | 12 year to Women's Small | 7" (18 cm) | 8½" (22 cm) | 85 yd (78 m) |
| **Size 3** | Women's Med. | 7½" (19 cm) | 9" (23 cm) | 95 yd (87 m) |
| **Size 4** | Women's Large/ Men's Small | 8" (20 cm) | 9½" (24 cm) | 115 yd (105 m) |
| **Size 5** | Men's Medium | 8½" (22 cm) | 10½" (27 cm) | 130 yd (119 m) |
| **Size 6** | Men's Large | 9" (23 cm) | 11½" (29 cm) | 145 yd (133 m) |

*Directions will be shown in the pattern as follows: Size 1 (Size 2, Size 3) (Size 4, Size 5, Size 6)*

# MITTEN POWER 3.5
### 3½ STITCHES = 1 INCH (2.5 CM)

### CAST ON STITCHES
### AND BEGIN KNITTING CUFF
Make both mittens alike.

Using smaller needles, cast on 20 (24, 24) (28, 28, 32)sts. Place BOR marker and join in the round being careful not to twist (see page 20).

**Round 1:** *K2, p2*; repeat from * to * to end of round.

Repeat round 1 until cuff measures 2" (2¼", 2½") (2¾", 2¾", 3") [5 (6, 6.5) (7, 7, 7.5) cm].

### THUMB GUSSET
Change to larger needles.

**Round 1:** Knit.

**Round 2 for sizes 1 and 2 only:** Inc 1, knit to end of round.

**Round 2 for all other sizes:** Knit.

**Round 3 for sizes 3, 4, 5, and 6 only:** Inc 1, knit to end of round. Skip for other sizes.

There should be:
21 (25, 25) (29, 29, 33) sts.

**Round 4:** Knit 10 (12, 12) (14, 14, 16) sts, pm, k1, pm, k to end of round.

**Round 5:** Knit to first marker, sm, M1L, k1, M1R, sm, k to end of round—3 sts between gusset markers.

**Round 6:** Knit to end of round, slipping markers as you come to them.

**Round 7:** Knit to first marker, sm, M1L, knit to next marker, M1R, sm, k to end of round—5 sts between markers.

**Round 8:** Repeat round 6.

**Round 9 for sizes 2, 3, 4, and 5 only:** Repeat round 6. Skip for other sizes.

**Round 10:** Knit to first marker, sm, M1L, knit to next marker, M1R, sm, k to end of round—7 sts between markers.

**Round 11:** Repeat round 6.

**Round 12 for sizes 1, 2, 3, 4, and 5 only:** Repeat round 6. Skip for other sizes.

**Round 13:** Knit to first marker, sm, M1L, knit to next marker, M1R, sm, k to end of round—9 sts between markers.

**Round 14:** Repeat round 6.

**Size 1, 2, and 3: Proceed to round 21.**

**Round 15 for sizes 4, 5, and 6 only:** Repeat round 6.

**Round 16 for sizes 4, 5, and 6 only:** Knit to first marker, sm, M1L, knit to next marker, M1R, sm, k to end of round—11 sts between markers.

**Rounds 17 for sizes 4, 5, and 6 only:** Repeat round 6 twice.

**Sizes 4 and 5: Proceed to round 21.**

**Round 18 for size 6 only:** Repeat round 6.

**Round 19 for size 6 only:** Knit to first marker, sm, M1L, knit to next marker, M1R, sm, k to end of round—13 sts between markers.

**Round 20 for size 6 only:** Repeat round 6.

**Round 21:** Knit to marker, remove marker, place next 9 (9, 9) (11, 11, 13) sts on holder, remove marker, use backward thumb loop to cast on 2 (1, 2) (1, 2, 1) sts over gap left by gusset stitches, k to end of round.

**Round 22:** Knit.

**Round 23 for size 2:** K12, k2tog, knit to end of round.

**Round 23 for size 4:** K14, k2tog, knit to end of round.

**Round 23 for size 6:** K16, k2tog, knit to end of round. Skip round 23 for sizes 1, 3 and 5.

**There should be:**
22 (24, 26) (28, 30, 32) sts.

**Round 24:** Knit.

Repeat round 24 until length from cuff is approximately 4¼" (4¾", 5") (5¾", 6", 6½") [11 (12, 12.5) (14.5, 15, 16.5) cm]. At this point, the total length from cast-on row should be 6¼" (7", 7½") (8", 8¾", 9½") [16 (18, 19) (20, 22, 24) cm].

### SHAPE TIP OF MITTEN

Work decreases to shape the tip of the mitten.

**Round 1 for sizes 2, 4, and 6 only:** Knit.

**Round 1 for size 1:** [Knit 9, k2tog] twice—20 sts remain.

**Round 1 for size 3:** [Knit 11, k2tog] twice—24 sts remain.

**Round 1 for size 5:** [Knit 13, k2tog] twice—28 sts remain.

**Round 2:** *Knit 3 (4, 4) (5, 5, 6) sts, k2tog*; repeat from * to * to end of round—16 (20, 20) (24, 24, 28) sts remain.

**Round 3:** Knit.

**Round 4:** *Knit 2 (3, 3) (4, 4, 5) sts, k2tog*; repeat from * to * to end of round—12 (16, 16) (20, 20, 24) sts remain.

**Round 5:** Knit.

**Round 6:** *Knit 1 (2, 2) (3, 3, 4) sts, k2tog*; repeat from * to * to end of round—8 (12, 12) (16, 16, 20) sts remain.

**Size 1: Proceed to round 11.**

**Round 7 for size 6 only:** Knit. Skip for other sizes.

**Round 8 for sizes 2, 3, 4, 5, and 6 only:** *Knit - (1, 1) (2, 2, 3) sts, k2tog*; repeat from * to * to end of round— - (8, 8) (12, 12, 16) sts remain.

**Size 2 and 3: Proceed to round 11.**

**Round 9 for sizes 4, 5, and 6 only:** *Knit - (-, -) (1, 1, 2) sts, k2tog*; repeat from * to * to end of round— - (-, -) (8, 8, 12) sts remain.

(continued)

**Size 4 and 5: Proceed to round 11.**
**Round 10 for size 6 only:** *K1, k2tog*; repeat from * to * to end of round— 8 sts remain.
**Round 11:** *K2tog*; repeat from * to * to end of round—4 sts remain.

## FINISHING MAIN PORTION OF MITTEN
Cut yarn leaving an 8" (20 cm) tail. Thread tail onto yarn needle and draw through remaining stitches on needle. Pull to tighten loop and pass yarn needle to inside of mitten and weave yarn tail through stitches to secure.

## MITTEN THUMB
Remove gusset stitches from stitch holder and distribute on three DPNs. Attach yarn leaving an 8" (20 cm) tail, pick up and knit 3 (3, 3) (4, 4, 4) stitches over gap. Place marker to indicate beginning of round, join in the round and continue to knit as follows:
**Round 1 for sizes 1, 2, and 3:** Knit until 4 sts remain before end of round, ssk, k1, k2tog (you will need to reposition the BOR marker to fall after the k2tog).
**Round 1 for sizes 5, 6, 7, and 8:** Knit until 5 sts remain before end of round, ssk, k2, k2tog (you will need to reposition the BOR marker to fall after the k2tog).
**There should be:**
10 (10, 10) (13, 13, 15) sts.
**Round 2:** Knit.
 Repeat round 2 for 6 (6, 8) (9, 10, 10) more rows or until length from beginning of thumb (where stitches were picked up over gusset space) equals 1¼" (1¼", 1½") (1¾", 2", 2") [3 (3 4) (4.5, 5, 5) cm].

## SHAPE TIP OF THUMB
Work decreases to taper tip of thumb.
**Round 1 for sizes 1, 2, 3, 4, and 5:** K2tog, knit to end of round.
**Round 1 for size 6:** Knit.
**There should be:** 9 (9, 9) (12, 12, 15) sts.
**Round 2:** *K1 (1, 1) (2, 2, 3), k2tog*; repeat from * to * to end of round–6 (6, 6) (9, 9, 12) sts remain.
**Round 3:** Knit.
**Size 1, 2 and 3: Proceed to round 7.**
**Round 5 for sizes 4, 5, and 6 only:** *Knit - (-, -) (1, 1, 2) sts, k2tog*; repeat from * to * to end of round— - (-, -) (6, 6, 9) sts remain.
**Size 4 and 5: Proceed to round 7.**
**Round 6 for size 6 only:** *K1, k2tog*; repeat from * to * to end of round— 6 sts remain.
**Round 7:** *K1, k2tog*—4 sts remain.

## FINISHING THUMB
Cut yarn leaving a tail at least 8" (20 cm) long. Thread tail onto yarn needle and draw through remaining stitches on needle. Pull to tighten loop and pass to inside of thumb and weave through stitches to secure. Using yarn tail at the base of the thumb, close any gaps that might remain and secure by weaving through stitches.
 Repeat directions for second mitten. To finish mittens weave in all ends and steam lightly.

## MITTEN POWER 2.5: Size, Finished Dimensions, and Yardage

| | To Fit Size | Finished Hand Circumference | Finished Length | Approximate Yardage |
|---|---|---|---|---|
| **Size 1** | 12 year to Women's Small | 7" (18 cm) | 8½" (22 cm) | 60 yd (55 m) |
| **Size 2** | Women's Med. | 7½" (19 cm) | 9" (23 cm) | 70 yd (64 m) |
| **Size 3** | Women's Large/ Men's Small | 8" (20 cm) | 9½" (24 cm) | 80 yd (73 m) |
| **Size 4** | Men's Medium | 8½" (22 cm) | 10½" (27 cm) | 90 yd (82 m) |
| **Size 5** | Men's Large | 9" (23 cm) | 11½" (29 cm) | 100 yd (91 m) |

*Directions will be shown in the pattern as follows: Size 1 (Size 2, Size 3, Size 4, Size 5)*

## MITTEN POWER 2.5

**2½ STITCHES = 1 INCH (2.5 CM)**

### CAST ON STITCHES AND BEGIN KNITTING CUFF

Make both mittens alike.

Using smaller needles, cast on 18 (18, 20, 20, 22) sts. Place BOR marker and join in the round being careful not to twist (see page 20).

**Round 1:** *K1, p1*; repeat from * to * to end of round.

Repeat round 1 until cuff measures 1¼" (1¼", 1½", 1½", 1¾") [3 (3, 4, 4, 4.5) cm].

### THUMB GUSSET

Change to larger needles.

**Rounds 1–3:** Knit.

**Round 4 for size 1:** Inc 1, knit to end of round.

**Round 4 for sizes 2, 3, 4, and 5:** Knit.

**Round 5 for sizes 2, 3, 4, and 5:** Inc 1, knit to end of round. Skip for other sizes.

(continued)

### GAUGE

10 sts and 16 rows = 4" (10 cm) in stockinette stitch

### YARN

Super bulky weight yarn; the approximate yardage for each size is shown in the chart above.

### NEEDLES AND NOTIONS

US size 15 (10 mm) double-pointed needles or size required to achieve gauge

US size 11 (8 mm) double-pointed needles (or two sizes smaller than size used to achieve gauge)

Optional Magic Loop: above needle sizes in a circular needle at least 32" (81 cm) long.

Circular stitch markers

Yarn needle for weaving in ends

**There should be:** 19 (19, 21, 21, 23) sts.

**Round 6:** Knit 9 (9, 10, 10, 11) sts, pm, k1, pm, k to end of round.

**Round 7:** Knit to first marker, sm, M1L, k1, M1R, sm, k to end of round—3 sts between gusset markers.

**Round 8:** Knit to end of round, slipping markers as you come to them.

**Round 9 for size 2 only:** Repeat round 8. Skip for other sizes.

**Round 10:** Knit to first marker, sm, M1L, knit to next marker, M1R, sm, k to end of round—5 sts between markers.

**Round 11:** Repeat round 8.

**Round 12 for sizes 1, 2, and 5 only:** Repeat round 8. Skip for other sizes.

**Round 13:** Knit to first marker, sm, M1L, knit to next marker, M1R, sm, k to end of round—7 sts between markers.

**Round 14:** Repeat round 8.

**Sizes 1 and 2: Proceed to round 18.**

**Round 15 for sizes 4, and 5 only:** Repeat round 8. Skip for other sizes.

**Round 16 for sizes 3, 4, and 5 only:** Knit to first marker, sm, M1L, knit to next marker, M1R, sm, k to end of round—9 sts between markers.

**Round 17 for sizes 3, 4, and 5 only:** Repeat round 8.

**Round 18:** Knit to marker, remove marker, place next 7 (7, 9, 9, 9) sts on holder, remove marker, use backward thumb loop to cast on 1 st over gap left by gusset stitches, k to end of round.

**Round 19:** Knit.

**Round 20 for size 1 only:** K9, k2tog, knit to end of round.

**Round 20 for size 3 only:** K10, k2tog, knit to end of round. Skip round 20 for sizes 2, 4 and 5.

**There should be:** 18 (19, 20, 21, 23) sts.

**Round 21:** Knit.

Repeat round 21 until length from cuff is approximately 5¾" (6¼", 6¾", 7¼", 7¾") [14.5 (16, 17, 18.5, 19.5) cm]. At this point, the total length from cast-on row should be 7" (7½", 8¼", 8¾", 9½") [18 (19, 21, 22, 24) cm].

### SHAPE TIP OF MITTEN

Work decreases to shape the tip of the mitten.

**Round 1 for size 1:** [Knit 7, k2tog] twice—16 sts remain.

**Round 1 for size 2:** [K3, k2tog] 3 times, k4—16 sts remain.

**Round 1 for size 3:** Knit.

**Round 1 for size 4:** K10, k2tog, knit to end of round, 20 sts remain.

**Round 1 for size 5:** [K4, k2tog] 3 times, k5, 20 sts remain.

**Round 2:** *Knit 2 (2, 3, 3, 3) sts, k2tog*; repeat from * to * to end of round—12 (12, 16, 16, 16) sts remain.

**Round 3:** Knit.

**Round 4:** *Knit 1 (1, 2, 2, 2) sts, k2tog*; repeat from * to * to end of round—8 (8, 12, 12 12) sts remain.

**Sizes 1 and 2: Proceed to round 7.**

**Round 5 for size 3, 4, and 5 only:** Knit.

**Round 6 for size 3, 4, and 5 only:** *K1, k2tog*; repeat from * to * to end of round—8 sts remain.

**Round 7:** *K2tog*; repeat from * to * to end of round—4 sts remain.

### FINISHING MAIN PORTION OF MITTEN

Cut yarn leaving an 8" (20 cm) tail. Thread tail onto yarn needle and draw through remaining stitches on needle. Pull to tighten loop and pass yarn needle to inside of mitten and weave yarn tail through stitches to secure.

## MITTEN THUMB

Remove gusset stitches from stitch holder and distribute on three DPNs.

Attach yarn leaving an 8" (20 cm)tail, pick up and knit 3 stitches over gap. Place marker to indicate beginning of round, join in the round and continue to knit as follows:

**Round 1:** Knit until 4 sts remain before end of round, ssk, k1, k2tog (you will need to reposition the BOR marker to fall after the k2tog).

**There should be:** 8 (8, 10, 10, 10) sts.

**Round 2:** Knit.

Repeat Round 2 for 5 (6, 7, 8, 8) more rows or until length from beginning of thumb (where stitches were picked up over gusset space) equals 1¼" (1½", 1¾", 2", 2") [3 (4, 4.5, 5, 5) cm].

## SHAPE TIP OF THUMB

Work decreases to taper tip of thumb.

**Round 1 for sizes 3, 4, and 5:** K2tog, knit to end of round. Skip round 1 for other sizes.

**There should be:** 8 (8, 9, 9, 9) sts.

**Round 2 for sizes 1 and 2:**
*K2tog*; repeat from * to * to end of round—4 sts remain.

**Round 2 for sizes 3, 4, and 5:**
*K1, k2tog*; repeat from * to * to end of round—6 sts remain.

**Round 3:** Knit.

**Sizes 1 and 2:** Proceed to directions for finishing thumb.

**Round 4 for sizes 3, 4, and 5 only:**
*K2tog*; repeat from * to * to end of round—3 sts remain.

## FINISHING THUMB

Cut yarn leaving a tail at least 8" (20 cm) long. Thread tail onto yarn needle and draw through remaining stitches on needle. Pull to tighten loop and pass to inside of thumb and weave through stitches to secure. Using yarn tail at the base of the thumb, close any gaps that might remain and secure by weaving through stitches.

Repeat directions for second mitten. To finish mittens weave in all ends and steam lightly.

# Mitten Gallery

Now that you've learned the basics of making mittens you'll be able to experiment with different yarns. I can't help myself—I love the huge range of mitten sizes! One of my treats is to make the same pattern in different sizes and colors. I'm also inspired by trying different yarn weights and fiber compositions. All of these examples follow the simple patterns in the Mitten Power section.

## ANY COLOR/ANY SIZE

In just about any yarn shop you will find that worsted weight yarn is available in the greatest variety. In one brand, alone my shop carries over one hundred different colors. It's fun to experiment with some of the subtle variations such as solid, heather, and tweed.

**Pattern:** 5 sts = 1" (2.5 cm)

**Size:** The large size pair, shown in blue/green tweed, is size 5, women's medium. The medium size pair, shown in gold heather, is size 3, 8 to 10 years. The small size pair, shown in solid aqua, is size 1, 2 to 4 years.

**Large size pair yarn:** Medium weight smooth yarn, 150 yd (137 m)

**Medium size pair yarn:** Medium weight smooth yarn, 100 yd (91 m)

**Small size pair yarn:** Medium weight smooth yarn, 60 yd (55 m)

**Shown:** Large size pair: Cascade Yarns *220 Wool*, 100% wool; 220 yd (201 m) per 3.5 oz (100 g) skein, color 9434, 1 skein

**Medium size pair:** Cascade Yarns *220 Wool*, 100% wool; 220 yd (201 m) per 3.5 oz (100 g) skein, color 4010, 1 skein

**Small size pair:** Cascade Yarns *220 Wool*, 100% wool; 220 yd (201 m) per 3.5 oz (100 g) skein, color 8908, 1 skein

# WARM AND COZY

Nothing feels better on a winter day than mittens made of thick yarn making your hands feel warm and cozy. This yarn has just enough mohair to add some fuzzy comfort to the warmth of merino.

**Pattern:** 3.5 sts = 1" (2.5 cm)

**Size:** The size shown is size 3, women's medium

**Yarn:** Bulky weight smooth yarn, 95 yd (87 m)

**Shown:** Rowan Cocoon, 80% merino wool, 20% kid mohair; 126 yd (115 m) per 3.5 oz (100 g) ball, color #816, Kiwi, 1 ball.

## INSTANT SUCCESS

If you've already made the hat out of super bulky yarn, then you know that just a movie or two is all that's required to make these mittens (okay, maybe an epic). With this heavy yarn, a simple k1, p1 ribbing for a few rows is all that's needed for a cuff. Hand-dyed yarns are simply charming, but the colors can be quirky and these mittens are the perfect example. Believe it or not, those are the same color! Instead of being dismayed by the color difference between the two balls, I decided to make the best of it and create some interest with a few stripes.

**Pattern:** 2.5 sts = 1" (2.5 cm)

**Variations:** A contrast shade was used for the ribbing and to put a stripe in the mittens and thumb.

**Size:** The size shown is size 2, women's medium

**Yarn:** Super bulky weight single ply yarn, 70 yd (64 m) total: 45 yd (41 m) green, 25 yd (23 m) pink

**Shown:** Malabrigo *Rasta*, 100% merino wool; 89 yd (81 m) per 5.25 oz (150 g) skein, color Arco Iris, 2 differently shaded skeins if color contrast desired.

# Mighty Minis

## Colorful Slip Stitch Hat and Mittens

A lively slip stitch pattern is used to make a colorful mitten and hat set for babies. This design is worked in five different colors of hand-dyed merino yarn. It's a great project for using up leftovers in your stash but splurge and buy five skeins. You're sure to fall in love with the pattern and will make it many times for the lucky babies in your life.

The mittens don't have thumbs, so they are easier to put on squirmy babies. For an added detail, attach a cord from mitten to mitten. Your friends will think you're a genius and the mittens will never get lost.

*Please make a gauge swatch before you start knitting! For best results make a gauge of the slip stitch pattern in the round—try casting on 40 stitches (any even number will do). If you choose to make a swatch that is knit flat, then follow the slip stitch pattern in rows (page 64).*

## GAUGE

20 sts = 4" (10 cm) in stockinette stitch

22 sts = 4" (10 cm) in slip stitch pattern

*The gauge is the same for both the hat and the mittens.*

## YARN

Medium weight smooth yarn, five colors. Total yardage needed is shown in chart below.

Shown: Dream in Color *Classy*, 100% merino wool; 250 yd (228 m) per 4 oz (112 g) skein, colors: Some Summer Sky, Giant Peach, Spring Tickle, Cool Fire, and Butter Peeps

## NEEDLES AND NOTIONS

For HAT: US size 7 (4.5 mm) 16" (40 cm) circular needle or size required to achieve gauge

For HAT and MITTENS: US size 7 (4.5 mm) double-pointed needles or size required to achieve gauge

For MITTENS: US size 5 (3.75 mm) double-pointed needles (or two sizes smaller than size used to achieve gauge)

Optional Magic Loop: circular needle in sizes above at least 40" (101 cm) long for HAT and 32" (81 cm) long for MITTENS

Circular stitch marker

Yarn needle for weaving in ends

## ABBREVIATIONS

SSP = Slip Stitch Pattern (page 64)

For all other abbreviations see page 144.

### COLORFUL SLIP STITCH HAT: Size, Finished Dimensions, and Yardage

| | To Fit Size | Finished Hat Circumference | Finished Hat Height | Approximate Yardage |
|---|---|---|---|---|
| **Size 1** | newborn to 6 months | 12" (30 cm) | 6¾" (17 cm) | 90 yd (82 m) |
| **Size 2** | 6 to 9 months | 14" (36 cm) | 7¼" (18 cm) | 100 yd (91 m) |
| **Size 3** | 12 to 18 months | 16" (41 cm) | 8" (20 cm) | 110 yd (101 m) |

*Directions will be shown in the pattern as follows: Size 1 (Size 2, Size 3)*

### SLIP STITCH PATTERN (SSP)

Note that exact colors aren't specified. You can follow the color pattern shown in the photos or make up your own. It isn't important to follow the same color pattern throughout—sometimes a "mistake" can be better than the original plan. Rather than cut the colors between rounds, bring the unused yarn along with you! When you reach the last stitch of round 1 of the SSP, pass the working yarn under the other strands before working the stitch. This will make a loop around the "bundle" of other colored yarns and bring them along as work progresses.

**Round 1:** Change color, knit.
**Round 2:** Purl.
**Round 3:** Change color, *knit 1, slip 1*, repeat from * to * until the end of the round.
**Round 4:** *Purl 1, wyib slip 1*, repeat from * to * until the end of the round.

Repeat Rounds 1 to 4 until desired length.

### SSP IN ROWS

If you are making a swatch that is knit flat (working back and forth instead of in the round) then work the rows as follows:

**Row 1:** Change color, knit.
**Row 2:** Knit.
**Row 3:** Change color, *knit 1, slip 1*, repeat from * to * until the end of the row.
**Row 4:** *K1, wyif slip 1*, repeat from * to * until the end of the row.

Repeat Rows 1 to 4 until desired length.

### STRIPE PATTERN

While following the slip stitch pattern (a four-round repeat), the color is changed every other round. In other words, each color is used for two rounds before changing to a new color. This design looks best when five colors are repeated in sequence. If you plan to use a different number of colors, keep in mind that an odd number of colors is best.

## COLORFUL SLIP STITCH HAT

### CAST ON STITCHES AND BEGIN KNITTING

Using circular needle, cast on 68 (76, 88) stitches. Place BOR marker and join in the round being careful not to twist (see page 20). Work two rows in rib as follows:

**Round 1:** *K2, p2*, repeat from * to * to end of round.
**Round 2:** Repeat round 1.

### START SLIP STITCH PATTERN

At this point you will change to a new color and begin the slip stitch pattern. Remember that the stitch pattern is repeated every four rounds and the color is changed every two rounds.

**Round 3:** SSP Round 1 to end of round.
**Round 4:** SSP Round 2 to end of round.
**Round 5:** SSP Round 3 to end of round.
**Round 6:** SSP Round 4 to end of round.

Continue to repeat the SSP rounds as established in rounds 3 to 6 until the beginning of the decrease section to shape the top of the hat.

### SHAPE TOP

Work decreases to shape the crown of the hat. Discontinue the SSP after SSP Round 4 is completed and the length from the cast-on row is 4½" (5", 5½") [11.5 (12.5, 14) cm]. Make the length from the cast-on edge a bit shorter or longer in order to complete the SSP through Round 4.

From this point on, work in stockinette stitch (all knit) and at the same time change colors every four rounds. If preferred, the top section can be made all in one color or any stripe sequence you would like.

Each size has unique directions for the first three rounds; after that the directions for all three sizes are the same. Change to DPNs when the stitches will no longer fit comfortably around the circular needle.

### SIZE 1
**Round 1:** Change color, knit.
**Round 2:** *Knit 15, k2tog*, repeat from * to * to end of round—64 sts remain.
**Round 3:** Knit.

### SIZE 2
**Round 1:** Change color, knit.
**Round 2:** *Knit 17, k2tog*, repeat from * to * to end of round—72 sts remain.
**Round 3:** Knit.

### SIZE 3
**Round 1:** Change color, knit.
**Round 2:** *Knit 9, k2tog*, repeat from * to * to end of round—80 sts remain.
**Round 3:** Knit.

### ALL SIZES
**Round 4:** *K6, k2tog*, repeat from * to * to end of round—56 (63, 70) sts remain.
**Round 5:** Change color, knit.
**Round 6:** *K5, k2tog*, repeat from * to * to end of round—48 (54, 60) sts remain.
**Round 7:** Knit.
**Round 8:** *K4, k2tog*, repeat from * to * to end of round—40 (45, 50) sts remain.
**Round 9:** Change color, knit.
**Round 10:** *K3, k2tog*, repeat from * to * to end of round—32 (36, 40) sts remain.
**Round 11:** Knit.
**Round 12:** *K2, k2tog*, repeat from * to * to end of round—24 (27, 30) sts remain.
**Round 13:** Change color, knit.
**Round 14:** *K1, k2tog*, repeat from * to * to end of round—16 (18, 20) sts remain.
**Round 15:** Knit.
**Round 16:** *K2tog*, repeat from * to * to end of round—8 (9, 10) sts remain.
**Round 17:** Change color, knit.
**Round 18 for size 1:** *K2tog*, repeat from * to * to end of round—4 sts remain.

**Round 18 for size 2:** *K2tog*, repeat from * to * until 1 st remains before end of round, k1—5 sts remain.
**Round 18 for size 3:** *K2tog*, repeat from * to * to end of round—5 sts remain.
**Round 19 for sizes 2 and 3 only:** K2tog, k to end of round—4 sts remain.

### MAKE I-CORD KNOT
Transfer stitches to a double-pointed needle. Knit all 4 stitches. **Do not turn the needle.** At the end of the row, instead of turning the needle to start a new row, push stitches from left side of needle to right side of needle. Start the new row by pulling the yarn across the back of stitches (1) to work the first stitch and knit all 4 stitches. Continue in same fashion, pushing the stitches back across the needle at the end of each row. Within a few rows, the knitting will begin to form into a tube. Work I-cord for approximately 2" to 3" (5 to 7.5 cm) depending on length of knot desired. Bind off 4 stitches and cut yarn. Work yarn invisibly into cord. Tie into knot.

1

### OPTIONAL PLAIN TOP WITHOUT I-CORD KNOT
After round 18 is completed, cut the yarn leaving a tail at least 8" (20 cm) long. Using a yarn needle, thread the tail through the remaining stitches and pass through the hole in the top of the hat to the inside. Pull the tail firmly to close the hole and weave the ends into the stitches on the inside of the hat to secure.

Weave in all other ends and steam lightly.

## COLORFUL SLIP STITCH MITTENS: Size, Finished Dimensions, and Yardage

| | To Fit Size | Finished Hand Circumference | Finished Mitten Length | Approximate Yardage |
|---|---|---|---|---|
| **Size 1** | newborn to 6 months | 5" (13 cm) | 3½" (9 cm) | 24 yd (22 m) |
| **Size 2** | 6 to 9 months | 5¼" (13 cm) | 4" (10 cm) | 25 yd (23 m) |
| **Size 3** | 12 to 18 months | 5½" (14 cm) | 4½" (11 cm) | 26 yd (24 m) |

*Directions will be shown in the pattern as follows: Size 1 (Size 2, Size 3)*

# COLORFUL SLIP STITCH MITTENS

### CAST ON STITCHES AND MAKE RIBBED CUFF

Right and left mittens are worked the same.

Using smaller needles, cast on 24 (28, 28) sts. Place BOR marker and join in the round being careful not to twist (see page 20).

**Round 1:** *K2, p2*; repeat from * to * to end of round.

Repeat round 1 until cuff measures 1" (2.5 cm).

Work final row of ribbing as follows for each size:

**Size 1:** *K2, p2, k1, kf&b, p2, k2, p1, p1f&b*, repeat from * to * one more time—28 sts.

**Size 2:** [K2, p2] three times, k1, kf&b, [p2, k2] three times, p1, pf&b—30 sts.

**Size 3:** K2, p2, k2, p1, pf&b, k2, p2, k1, kf&b, p2, k2, p2, k1, kf&b, p2, k2, p1, pf&b—32 sts.

### MAIN PORTION OF MITTEN

At this point you will change to a new color and begin the Slip Stitch pattern. Remember that the stitch pattern is repeated every four rows and the color is changed every two rows.

Change to larger needles.

**Round 1:** SSP Round 1 to end of round.
**Round 2:** SSP Round 2 to end of round.
**Round 3:** SSP Round 3 to end of round.
**Round 4:** SSP Round 4 to end of round.

Continue to repeat the Slip Stitch Pattern rounds as established in rounds 1–4 until the beginning of the decrease section to shape the tip of the mitten.

### SHAPE TIP OF MITTEN

Work decreases to shape the tip of the mittens. Discontinue the SSP after SSP Round 4 is completed and the length from the cast-on row is 3" (3½", 4") [7.5 (9, 10) cm]. Make the length from cast-on edge a little shorter or longer in order to complete the SSP through Round 4. From this point on, knit all sts. working decreases as indicated and working remaining rows in the same color.

**Round 1:** Change color, knit
**Round 2:** *K2tog*; repeat from * to * to end of round—14 (15, 16) sts remain.
**Round 3 for sizes 1 and 3 only:** *K2tog*; repeat from * to * to end of round—7 (-, 8) sts remain.
**Round 3 for size 2 only:** *K2 tog*; repeat from * to * until 1 st remains, k1—8 sts remain.

**FINISHING MAIN PORTION OF MITTEN**
Cut yarn leaving an 8" (20 cm) tail.
Thread tail onto yarn needle and draw
through remaining stitches on needle.
Pull to tighten loop and pass yarn needle
to inside of mitten and weave yarn tail
through stitches to secure.

Repeat directions for other mitten.
Weave in all ends and steam lightly.

# Baby Cable Hat

Simple yet elegant; that's the essence of this beautiful baby hat. Even a newborn can wear a hat made from this soft organic cotton yarn. The elegant cable pattern is simple and quick to make. If you're at the age like I am when all of my kids' friends are having babies, then make a collection of these hats and keep them on hand for last minute gifts.

## GAUGE

16 sts = 4" (10 cm) in stockinette stitch

18 sts = 4" (10 cm) in cable pattern

## YARN

Bulky weight nubby yarn; the approximate yardage for each size is shown in the chart below.

Shown: Classic Elite Yarns *Verde Collection Sprout*, 100% cotton; 109 yd (100 m) per 3.5 oz (100 g) skein, color 4354 Pea Blossom, 1 skein.

## NEEDLES AND NOTIONS

US size 10 (6 mm) 16" (40 cm) circular needle* or size required to achieve gauge

US size 8 (5 mm) 16" (40 cm) circular needle* (or two sizes smaller than size used to achieve gauge)

US size 10 (6 mm) double-pointed needles or size required to achieve gauge

*If you prefer the smaller sizes can be worked on a 12" (30 cm) circular needle or entirely with double-pointed needles.

Optional Magic Loop: above needle sizes in a circular needle at least 40" (101 cm) long.

Cable needle

Circular stitch marker

Yarn needle for weaving in ends

## ABBREVIATIONS

4-st RKC = Slip next 2 sts purlwise to cable needle and hold at back of work, knit next 2 sts from left needle, then knit 2 sts from cable needle

## BABY CABLE HAT: Size, Finished Dimensions, and Yardage

|  | To Fit Size | Finished Hat Circumference | Finished Hat Height | Approximate Yardage |
|---|---|---|---|---|
| Size 1 | newborn to 6 months | 12½" (32 cm) | 6" (15 cm) | 90 yd (82 m) |
| Size 2 | 6 to 9 months | 14" (36 cm) | 7" (18 cm) | 100 yd (91 m) |
| Size 3 | 12 to 18 months | 16" (41 cm) | 8" (20 cm) | 110 yd (101 m) |

*Directions will be shown in the pattern as follows: Size 1 (Size 2, Size 3)*

## BABY CABLE
## HAT

### CAST ON STITCHES
### AND BEGIN KNITTING

Using smaller circular needle, cast on 56 (64, 72) stitches. Place BOR marker and join in the round being careful not to twist (see page 21).

**Round 1:** *K4, p4*; repeat from * to * to end of round.

**Rounds 2–3:** Repeat round 1 twice.

Change to larger circular needle for remainder of hat.

**Rounds 4–6:** Repeat round 1 three times.

**Round 7:** *4-st RKC, p4*; repeat from * to * to end of round.

**Rounds 8–12:** *K4, p4*; repeat from * to * to end of round.

**Round 13:** *4-st RKC, p4*; repeat from * to * to end of round.

**Rounds 14–19:** Repeat rounds 8–13.

**Size 1: Proceed to round 32.**

**Rounds 20–25 for sizes 2 and 3 only:** Repeat rounds 8–13.

**Size 2: Proceed to round 32.**

**Rounds 26–31 for size 3 only:** Repeat rounds 8–13.

All sizes continue alike.

**Rounds 32–33:** *K4, p4*; repeat from * to * to end of round.

**Round 34:** *K4, p2tog, p2*; repeat from * to * to end of round—49 (56, 63) sts remain.

**Round 35:** *K4, p3*; repeat from * to * to end of round.

**Round 36:** *K4, p1, p2tog*; repeat from * to * to end of round—42 (48, 54) sts remain.

**Round 37:** *4-st RKC, p2*; repeat from * to * to end of round.

**Round 38:** *K4, p2tog*; repeat from * to * to end of round—35 (40, 45) sts remain.

**Round 39:** *K4, p1*; repeat from * to * to end of round.

**Round 40:** *K2tog, k2, p1*; repeat from * to * to end of round—28 (32, 36) sts remain.

**Round 41:** *K2tog, k1, p1*; repeat from * to * to end of round—21 (24, 27) sts remain.

**Round 42:** *K2tog, p1*; repeat from * to * to end of round—14 (16, 18) sts remain.

**Round 43:** *Ssk*; repeat from * to * to end of round, 7 (8, 9) sts remain.

To finish the hat, cut the yarn leaving a tail at least 8" (20 cm) long. Using a yarn, needle thread the tail through the remaining stitches and pass through the hole in the top of the hat to the inside. Pull the tail firmly to close the hole and weave the ends into the stitches on the inside of the hat to secure.

Weave in all other ends and steam lightly.

# Hot Air Balloon Hat and Mittens

You might wonder about the title. When I finished this hat I couldn't help but think about a hot air balloon. I thought the look was so cute, I gave the mittens a pointed tip too. The no-thumb mittens are easy to put on a baby. You'll find that the superwash wool is amazingly soft and perfectly suitable for even the youngest babies. Any worsted weight yarn would be suitable for this pattern.

## GAUGE

19 sts = 4" (10 cm) in stockinette stitch

*The gauge is the same for both the hat and the mittens.*

## YARN

Medium weight smooth yarn; the approximate yardage for each size is shown in the charts

Shown: Lorna's Laces *Shepherd Worsted,* 100% wool; 225 yd (206 m)

per 4 oz (112 g) skein, color 601 Rainbow, 1 skein.

Only one skein is needed for both the hat and the mittens.

## NEEDLES AND NOTIONS

For HAT: US size 7 (4.5 mm) 16" (40 cm) circular needle* or size required to achieve gauge

US size 6 (4 mm) 16" (40 cm) circular needle* (or one size smaller than size used to achieve gauge)

For HAT and MITTENS: US size 7 (4.5 mm) double-pointed needles or size required to achieve gauge

FOR MITTENS: US size 6 (4 mm) double-pointed needles (or one size smaller than size used to achieve gauge)

*Smaller size hats can be worked on a 12" (30 cm) circular needle or entirely with double-pointed needles.

Optional Magic Loop: circular needle in sizes above, at least 40" (101 cm) long for HAT and at least 32" (81 cm) long for MITTENS

Circular stitch marker

Small stitch holder (or waste yarn) for MITTENS

Yarn needle for weaving in ends

## HOT AIR BALLOON HAT: Size, Finished Dimensions, and Yardage

|  | To Fit Size | Finished Hat Circumference | Finished Hat Height | Approximate Yardage |
|---|---|---|---|---|
| **Size 1** | newborn to 6 months | 12" (30 cm) | 7" (18 cm) | 85 yd (78 m) |
| **Size 2** | 6 to 9 months | 14" (36 cm) | 8" (20 cm) | 90 yd (82 m) |
| **Size 3** | 12 to 18 months | 16" (41 cm) | 9" (23 cm) | 95 yd (87 m) |

*Directions will be shown in the pattern as follows: Size 1 (Size 2, Size 3)*

# HOT AIR BALLOON HAT

## CAST ON STITCHES AND BEGIN KNITTING

Using smaller circular needle, cast on 54 (66, 78) stitches. Place BOR marker and join in the round being careful not to twist (see page 20).

**Round 1:** *K3, p3*; repeat from * to * to end of round.

Repeat round 1 until length from cast-on row is 1" (2.5 cm).

Change to larger needles and adjust stitch count as follows:

**Round 1 size 1 only:** [K26, kf&b] twice.
**Round 1 size 2 only:** Knit.
**Round 1 size 3 only:** [K37, k2tog] twice.
**There should be:** 56 (66, 76 sts).
**Round 2:** Knit.

Repeat round 2 until length from cast-on edge is 4½" (5½", 6½") [11.5 (14, 16.5) cm].

## SHAPE TOP

Work decreases to shape the crown of the hat. Notice that the larger sizes require more rows to decrease their greater number of stitches. If you are making one of the smaller sizes then skip the beginning rows that don't apply to your hat. Change to DPNs when the stitches will no longer fit comfortably around the circular needle.

**Round 1 for size 3 only:** *K17, k2tog*; repeat from * to * to end of round—72 sts remain.

**Round 2 for size 3 only:** *K7, k2tog*; repeat from * to * to end of round—64 sts remain.

**Round 3 for size 2 only:** [K31, k2tog] twice—64 sts remain.

**Round 3 for size 3 only:** Knit.

**Round 4 for sizes 2 and 3:** *K6, k2tog*; repeat from * to * to end of round—56 sts remain.

**Round 5 for sizes 2 and 3:** Knit.

From this point all sizes are worked the same.

**Round 6:** *K5, k2tog*; repeat from * to * to end of round—48 sts remain.

**Rounds 7–8:** Knit.

**Round 9:** *K4, k2tog*; repeat from * to * to end of round—40 sts remain.

**Rounds 10–11:** Knit.

**Round 12:** *K3, k2tog*; repeat from * to * to end of round—32 sts remain.

**Rounds 13–14:** Knit.

**Round 15:** *K2, k2tog*; repeat from * to * to end of round—24 sts remain.

**Rounds 16–18:** Knit.

**Round 19:** *K1, k2tog*; repeat from * to * to end of round—16 sts remain.

**Rounds 20–22:** Knit.

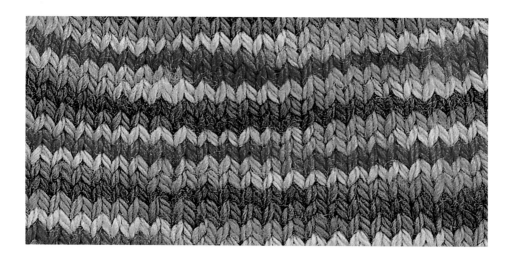

**Round 23:** *K2tog*; repeat from * to * to end of round—8 sts remain.
**Round 24:** Knit.
**Round 25:** K2tog until 4 sts remain.
To finish the hat, cut the yarn leaving a tail at least 8" (20 cm) long. Using a yarn needle, thread the tail through the remaining stitches and pass through the hole in the top of the hat to the inside. Pull the tail firmly to close the hole and weave the ends into the stitches on the inside of the hat to secure.

Weave in all other ends and steam lightly.

## HOT AIR BALLOON MITTENS: Size, Finished Dimensions, and Yardage

| | To Fit Size | Finished Hand Circumference | Finished Mitten Height | Approximate Yardage |
|---|---|---|---|---|
| **Size 1** | newborn to 6 months | 5¼" (13 cm) | 4" (10 cm) | 33 yd (30 m) |
| **Size 2** | 6 to 9 months | 5½" (14 cm) | 4½" (11 cm) | 35 yd (32 m) |
| **Size 3** | 12 to 18 months | 5¾" (15 cm) | 5" (13 cm) | 37 yd (34 m) |

*Directions will be shown in the pattern as follows: Size 1 (Size 2, Size 3)*

## HOT AIR BALLOON MITTENS

### CAST ON STITCHES AND BEGIN KNITTING CUFF

Make both mittens alike.

Using smaller needles, cast on 20 (24, 28) sts. Join in the round being careful not to twist, and place marker to indicate the beginning of the round (see page 20).

**Round 1:** *K2, p2*; repeat from * to * to end of round.

Repeat round 1 until cuff measures 1" (2.5 cm) from cast-on edge.

### MAIN PART OF MITTEN

Change to larger needles and adjust sts as follows:

**Round 1 for size 1 only:** *K4, kf&b*; repeat from * to * to end of round.

**Round 1 for size 2 only:** [K11, kf&b] twice.

**Round 1 for size 3 only:** Knit.

**There should be:** 24 (26, 28) sts.

**Round 2:** Knit.

Repeat round 2 until length from cast-on edge is 2¾" (3", 3¼") [7 (7.5, 8) cm].

### SHAPE TIP OF MITTEN

**Round 1 for size 2:** [K11, k2tog] twice—24 sts remain.

**Round 1 for sizes 1 and 3:** Knit.

**Round 2:** *K4 (4, 5), k2tog*; repeat from * to * to end of round—20 (20, 24) sts remain.

**Round 3:** Knit.

**Round 4:** *K3, (3, 4), k2tog*; repeat from * to * to end of round—16 (16, 20) sts remain.

**Round 5:** Knit.

**Round 6:** *K2 (2, 3), k2tog*; repeat from * to * to end of round—12 (12, 16) sts remain.

**Round 7:** *K1 (1, 2), k2tog*; repeat from * to * to end of round—8 (8, 12) sts remain.

**Sizes 1 and 2: Proceed to round 9.**

**Round 8 for size 3 only:** *K1, k2tog*; repeat from * to * to end of round— 8 sts remain.

**Round 9:** *K2tog*; repeat from * to * to end of round—4 sts remain.

Cut yarn leaving a tail at least 8" (20 cm) long. Thread tail onto yarn needle and draw through remaining stitches on needle. Pull to tighten loop and pass yarn needle to inside of mitten and weave yarn tail through stitches to secure.

Repeat directions for second mitten. To finish mittens, weave in all ends and steam lightly.

# Shout Out Loud Hat

I originally made this hat in earth tones. The subtle colors reminded me of a quiet walk in the woods. When I put the second set of colors together, I thought this is like shouting out loud compared to the first hat. Add the wild tassel on top of these vibrant colors and you have a hat for the most exuberant baby on the block! Who would guess that the wool and alpaca boucle could make a hat that's also soft as a cloud?

## GAUGE

16 sts = 4" (10 cm) in stockinette stitch

18 sts = 4" (10 cm) in 10-row color pattern

## YARN

Yarn A (Red): Medium weight thick and thin, nubby yarn 80 yd (73 m)

Yarn B (Green): Medium weight thick and thin, nubby yarn 15 yd (14 m)

Yarn C (Teal): Medium weight thick and thin, nubby yarn 10 yd (9 m)

Yarn D (Purple): Medium weight thick and thin, nubby yarn 15 yd (14 m)

Shown: Nashua Handknits *Paradise*, 48% cotton, 48% alpaca, 4% nylon; 87 yd (80 m) per 1.75 oz (50 g) skein

Yarn A: #2055, Deep Red

Yarn B: #1641, Dusty Teal

Yarn C: #1265, Spring Leaf

Yarn D: #1800, Violet

## NEEDLES AND NOTIONS

US size 10 (6 mm) 16" (40 cm) circular needle or size required to achieve gauge

US size 8 (5 mm) 16" (40 cm) circular needle (or two sizes smaller than size used to achieve gauge)

US size 10 (6 mm) double-pointed needles or size required to achieve gauge

Optional Magic Loop: above needle sizes in a circular needle at least 40" (101 cm) long

Circular stitch marker

Yarn needle for weaving in ends

The pattern combines an easy slip stitch with a simple 2-stitch Fair Isle pattern. Since the bouclé yarn hides any inconsistency in your tension it's an excellent project for gaining confidence with both techniques. You can substitute other yarns for this pattern by choosing a soft yarn that normally knits to a gauge of 15 or 16 stitches over 4" (10 cm).

## SHOUT OUT LOUD HAT: Size and Finished Dimensions

|  | To Fit Size | Finished Hat Circumference | Finished Hat Height |
|---|---|---|---|
| Size | 6 to 9 months | 14" (35.5 cm) | 7½" (19 cm) with brim folded |

*The finished size can be varied by using a smaller or larger needle and adding or subtracting length.*

## SHOUT OUT LOUD
## HAT

### CAST ON STITCHES
### AND BEGIN KNITTING

Using smaller circular needle and yarn A, cast on 64 stitches. Place BOR marker and join in the round being careful not to twist (see page 20).

**Round 1:** *K2, p2*; repeat from * to * to end of round.

Repeat round 1 until length from cast-on edge is 2½" (6.5 cm).

### START COLOR PATTERN

When not using a particular color allow it to hang on the inside of the hat. When resuming knitting with that color be sure to allow a bit of slack on the first stitch so it doesn't pull up the prior rows on which it was used.

Change to larger needle and work color pattern as follows:

**Round 1:** With yarn A, knit.
**Round 2:** *With yarn A, k1, with yarn B, k1*; repeat from * to * to end of round.
**Round 3:** With yarn A, knit.
**Round 4:** With yarn C, *k2, sl2*; repeat from * to * to end of round.
**Round 5:** Repeat round 4.
**Round 6:** With yarn A, knit.
**Round 7:** *With yarn A, k1, with yarn B, k1*; repeat from * to * to end of round.
**Round 8:** With yarn A, knit.
**Round 9:** With yarn D, *sl2, k2*; repeat from * to * to end of round.
**Round 10:** Repeat round 9.

Repeat rounds 1–10 until the length from the cast-on edge is 7" (18 cm) and you have just completed row 10.

### SHAPE TOP

Work decreases to shape the crown of the hat. When placing markers in round 1 choose a common color for all three markers that is different from the BOR marker.

**Round 1:** With yarn A, [k16, pm] 3 times, k to end of round.
**Round 2:** *With yarn A, k1, with yarn B, k1*; repeat from * to * to end of round.
**Round 3:** With yarn A, *ssk, k2tog, k12*; repeat from * to * to end of round—56 sts remain.
**Round 4:** With yarn C, *k2, sl2*; repeat from * to * to end of round.
**Round 5:** Repeat round 4.
**Round 6:** With yarn A, *ssk, k2tog, k10*; repeat from * to * to end of round—48 sts remain.
**Round 7:** *With yarn A, k1, with yarn B, k1*; repeat from * to * to end of round.
**Round 8:** With yarn A, *ssk, k2tog, k8*; repeat from * to * to end of round—40 sts remain.
**Round 9:** With yarn D, *sl2, k2*; repeat from * to * to end of round.
**Round 10:** Repeat round 9.
**Round 11:** With yarn A, *k2tog, k3*; repeat from * to * to end of round—32 sts remain.
**Round 12:** *With yarn A, k1, with yarn B, k1*; repeat from * to * to end of round.
**Round 13:** With yarn A, *k2tog, k2*; repeat from * to * to end of round—24 sts remain.
**Round 14:** With yarn C, *k2, sl2*; repeat from * to * to end of round.
**Round 15:** Repeat round 4.

Discontinue other colors and finish hat with yarn A.

**Round 16:** *K2tog, k1*; repeat from * to * to end of round—16 sts remain.
**Round 17:** Knit.
**Round 18:** *K2tog*' repeat from * to * to end of round—8 sts remain.

To finish the hat, cut the yarn leaving a tail at least 8" (20 cm) long. Using a yarn needle thread the tail through the remaining stitches and pass through the hole in the top of the hat to the inside.

Pull the tail firmly to close the hole and weave the ends into the stitches on the inside of the hat to secure.

Weave in all other ends and steam lightly.

**MAKE TASSEL**

Cut a piece of cardboard about 3½" (9 cm) square. Holding all four colors together wrap around cardboard eight times. Using a 1-yard (1 m) strand of yarn, tie a knot around the midpoint of all the strands on the cardboard (on the opposite side from where the wraps started). The ends of the knot should be uneven with one end being about 10" (25.5 cm); thread the long end onto a yarn needle. Use scissors to cut one end of the wraps (the same end where you began). Fold the bundle of strands and use the longer end of the knotted yarn to wrap around the bundle several times just below the fold. Pass the needle under the wraps and bring it up to meet the short end of the knotted yarn and tie an overhand knot with the two strands. Use the ends from the knot to attach the tassel to top of hat. Finish by weaving in ends on inside of hat.

# Simply Striped Hat and Mittens

I get really excited by color and when I first saw this yarn I fell in love with the subtle blending of color and different fibers. The yarn is basically a smooth single ply, but every so often an uneven nub of silk gives it a hand-spun look. The simple stripe design allows the colors to enhance each other while still showing off the rustic beauty of the yarn. The ribbed border with a mini cable adds a bit of unexpected texture.

This pattern is written for an Aran weight yarn which knits at 4.5 stitches per inch, a very common weight. Experiment with your own choices of yarn and stripe sequences. Of course, you can choose to knit the entire hat from a single color. Also, the rib can be knit as a k2, p2 rib without the mini cable.

## GAUGE

18 sts and 26 rows = 4" (10cm) in stockinette stitch

*The gauge is the same for both the hat and the mittens.*

## YARN

Medium weight smooth

For HAT:

Yarn A: HAT: 65 (70, 75) yd [59 (64, 69) m]

Yarn B: 35 (40, 45) yd [32 (37, 41) m]

Yarn C: 35 (40, 45) yd [32 (37, 41) m]

For MITTENS:

Yarn A: 50 (55, 60) yd [46 (50, 55) m]

Yarn B: 35 (38, 42) yd [32 (35, 38) m]

Yarn C: 35 (38, 42) yd [32 (35, 38) m]

Shown: The Fibre Company *Terra*, 48% baby alpaca, 40% wool, 20% silk; 98 yd (90 m) per 1.75 oz (50 g) ball

For HAT or MITTENS:

Yarn A: African Violet, 1 ball

Yarn B: Dark Indigo, 1 ball

Yarn C: Woad Light, 1 ball

To make both HAT and MITTENS: 2 balls of yarn A and one each of yarns B and C

## NEEDLES AND NOTIONS

For HAT: US size 8 (5 mm) 16" (40 cm) circular needle or size required to achieve gauge

US size 7 (4.5 mm) 16" (40 cm) circular needle (or one size smaller than size used to achieve gauge) if you plan to make an edge of ribbing or garter stitch

For HAT and MITTENS: US size 8 (5 mm) double-pointed needles or size required to achieve gauge

For MITTENS: US size 7 (4.5 mm) double-pointed needles (or one size smaller than size used to achieve gauge)

Optional Magic Loop: circular needle in sizes above, at least 40" (101 cm) long for HAT and at least 32" (81 cm) long for MITTENS.

Circular stitch marker

Small stitch holder (or waste yarn)

Yarn needle for weaving in ends

Optional: 2½" (6 cm) pom pom maker

## ABBREVIATIONS

2-st RT = K2tog but don't take the stitches off the left needle (there will be one new stitch on the right needle). Insert right needle into first stitch on left needle, knit it and then remove both stitches from left needle. Two new stitches have been formed on the right needle and the stitch count remains the same.

For all other abbreviations see Knitting Abbreviation Section, page 144.

## STRIPE PATTERN

Both the hat and the mittens use the same stripe pattern which begins after the mini cable rib is completed. Follow the stripe pattern at right at the same time as working the stitch pattern and shaping in the individual patterns. Plan ahead when you reach the top of the hat and the tip of the mittens and thumb. Don't leave a stripe that is any less than two rows high. You may have to shorten the previous stripe or lengthen the last stripe to accomplish this.

**Rounds 1–3:** Yarn B
**Rounds 4–8:** Yarn C
**Rounds 9–11:** Yarn A
**Rounds 12–16:** Yarn B
**Rounds 17–19:** Yarn C
**Round 20–24:** Yarn A

## SIMPLY STRIPED HAT: Size and Finished Dimensions

|        | To Fit Size  | Finished Hat Circumference | Finished Hat Height* |
|--------|--------------|----------------------------|----------------------|
| Size 1 | Adult Small  | 19½" (50 cm)               | 8" (20 cm)           |
| Size 2 | Adult Medium | 21¼" (54 cm)               | 8½" (22 cm)          |
| Size 3 | Adult Large  | 23" (58 cm)                | 9" (23 cm)           |

*Hat height does not include pom pom. Directions will be shown in the pattern as follows: Size 1 (Size 2, Size 3)*

# SIMPLY STRIPED HAT

### CAST ON STITCHES AND BEGIN KNITTING

Using smaller circular needle and yarn A, cast on 88 (96, 104) stitches. Place BOR marker and join in the round being careful not to twist (see page 20).

**Round 1:** *K2, p2*; repeat from * to * to end of round.

**Rounds 2–3:** Repeat round 1.

**Round 4:** * 2-st RT, p2*; repeat from * to * to end of round.

**Rounds 5–8:** Repeat rounds 1–4.

**Round 9:** *K1, M1L, ssk, p1*; repeat from * to * to end of round.

**Round 10:** *K3, p1*; repeat from * to * to end of round.

**Round 11:** K1, *M1R, k2, k2tog*; repeat from * to * to end of round. *(Note: remove the BOR marker before the k2tog at the end of the round and reposition it before the last k2tog).*

**Round 12:** Change to larger circular needle and knit to end of round.

**Round 13:** Begin stripe pattern and knit to end of round.

Repeat Round 13 until hat measures 5" (5½", 6") [12.5 (14, 15) cm] from the cast-on edge.

### TIP

An unsightly consequence of knitting stripes in the round is a ragged jog that occurs at the end of the round when colors are changed. This occurs because the last stitch of the round is actually one row higher than the first stitch of the round. To avoid this problem, knit the first round of the new color, slip the marker, and then lift the stitch of old color from below the first stitch of the new round and knit it together with the first stitch.

## SHAPE TOP

Work decreases to shape the crown of the hat. Notice that the larger sizes require more rows to decrease their greater number of stitches. If you are making one of the smaller sizes, then skip the rows that don't apply to your hat size. Change to DPNs when the stitches will no longer fit comfortably around the circular needle.

**Round 1 for size 3 only:** *K11, k2tog*; repeat from * to * to end of round— 96 sts remain.

**Round 2 for size 3 only:** Knit.

**Round 3 for sizes 2 and 3 only:** *K10, k2tog*; repeat from * to * to end of round—88 sts remain.

**Round 4 for sizes 2 and 3 only:** Knit.

(continued)

From this point all sizes are worked identically.

**Round 5:** *K9, k2tog*; repeat from * to * to end of round—80 sts remain.

**Round 6:** Knit.

**Round 7:** *K8, k2tog*; repeat from * to * to end of round—72 sts remain.

**Round 8:** Knit.

**Round 9:** *K7, k2tog*; repeat from * to * to end of round—64 sts remain.

**Round 10:** Knit.

**Round 11:** *K6, k2tog*; repeat from * to * to end of round—56 sts remain.

**Round 12:** Knit.

**Round 13:** *K5, k2tog*; repeat from * to * to end of round—48 sts remain.

**Round 14:** Knit.

**Round 15:** *K4, k2tog*; repeat from * to * to end of round—40 sts remain.

**Round 16:** Knit.

**Round 17:** *K3, k2tog*; repeat from * to * to end of round—32 sts remain.

**Round 18:** Knit.

**Round 19:** *K2, k2tog*; repeat from * to * to end of round—24 sts remain.

**Round 20:** Knit.

**Round 21:** *K1, k2tog*; repeat from * to * to end of round—16 sts remain.

**Round 22:** Knit.

**Round 23:** *K2tog*; repeat from * to * to end of round—8 sts remain.

To finish the hat, cut the yarn leaving a tail at least 8" (20 cm) long. Using a yarn needle, thread the tail through the remaining stitches and pass through the hole in the top of the hat to the inside. Pull the tail firmly to close the hole and weave the ends into the stitches on the inside of the hat to secure.

Make optional pom pom following directions on pom pom maker package. Steam lightly and attach pom pom if desired.

## SIMPLY STRIPED MITTENS: Size and Finished Dimensions

|  | To Fit Size | Finished Hand Circumference | Finished Mitten Height* |
|---|---|---|---|
| **Size 1** | Adult Small | 7" (18 cm) | 8½" (22 cm) |
| **Size 2** | Adult Medium | 7½" (19 cm) | 9" (23 cm) |
| **Size 3** | Adult Large | 8" (20 cm) | 10" (25 cm) |

*Directions will be shown in the pattern as follows: Size 1 (Size 2, Size3)*

## SIMPLY STRIPED MITTENS

### CAST ON STITCHES AND BEGIN KNITTING

Right and left mittens are worked the same.

Using smaller needle and yarn A, cast on 32 (32, 36) stitches. Place BOR marker and join in the round being careful not to twist (see page 20).

**Round 1:** *K2, p2*; repeat from * to * to end of round.

**Rounds 2–3:** Repeat round 1.

**Round 4:** * 2-st RT, p2*; repeat from * to * to end of round.

**Rounds 5–8:** Repeat rounds 1–4.

**Round 9:** *K1, M1L, ssk, p1*; repeat from * to * to end of round.

**Round 10:** *K3, p1*; repeat from * to * to end of round.

**Round 11:** K1, *M1R, k2, k2tog*; repeat from * to * to end of round. *(Note: remove the BOR marker before the k2tog at the end of the round and reposition it before the last k2tog).*

Change to larger needle and work round 12 as follows:

**Round 12 for sizes 1 and size 3 only:** Inc 1, knit to end of round.

**Round 12 for size 2 only:** Inc 1, k15, inc 1, knit to end of round.

**There should be:** 33 (34, 37) sts.

## MAKE GUSSET FOR THUMB

Begin stripe pattern.

**Round 13:** K16 (17, 18), pm, k1, pm, knit to end of round.

**Round 14:** K16 (17, 18), sm, M1L, k1, M1R, sm, knit to end of round—3 sts between markers.

**Round 15:** Knit to end of round, slipping markers as you come to them.

**Round 16 for size 1 only:** Knit. Skip for other sizes.

**Round 17:** K16 (17, 18), sm, M1L, k until next marker, M1R, sm, knit to end of round—5 sts between markers.

**Round 18:** Repeat round 15.

**Round 19 for sizes 1 and 3 only:** Knit. Skip for other sizes.

**Round 20:** K16 (17, 18), sm, M1L, k until next marker, M1R, sm, knit to end of round—7 sts between markers.

**Rounds 21–22:** Repeat round 15.

**Round 23:** K16 (17, 18), sm, M1L, k until next marker, M1R, sm, knit to end of round—9 sts between markers.

**Rounds 24–25:** Repeat round 15.

**Size 1: Proceed to round 32.**

**Round 26 for sizes 2 and 3 only:** Knit - (17, 18), sm, M1L, k until next marker, M1R, sm, knit to end of round— 11 sts between markers.

**Round 27–28 for sizes 2 and 3 only:** Repeat round 15.

**Size 2: Proceed to round 32.**

**Round 29 for size 3 only:** Knit - (-, 18), sm, M1L, k until next marker, M1R, sm, knit to end of round— 13 sts between markers.

**Round 30–31 for size 3 only:** Repeat round 15.

**Round 32:** Knit to marker, remove marker, place next 9 (11, 13) sts on holder, remove marker, use backwards thumb loop to cast on 1 (2, 2) sts over gap left by gusset stitches, k to end of round.

**Round 33:** Knit.

**Round 34:** K15 (16, 17), k2tog, knit to end of round. You should have 32 (34, 37) sts.

**Round 35:** Knit.

Repeat row 35 until length from cast-on row is 4½" (5 ", 5½") [11.5 (12.5, 14) cm].

## SHAPE TIP OF MITTEN

Work decreases to shape the tip of the mittens.

**Round 1 for size 1 only:** Knit.

**Round 1 for size 2 only:** [K15, k2tog] twice—32 sts remain.

**Round 1 for size 3 only:** K16, k2tog, knit to end of round—36 sts remain.

**Round 2:** *K6 (6, 7), k2tog*; repeat from * to * to end of round— 28 (28, 32) sts remain.

**Round 3:** Knit.

**Round 4:** *K5 (5, 6), k2tog*; repeat from * to * to end of round— 24 (24, 28) sts remain.

**Round 5:** Knit.

**Round 6:** *K4 (4, 5), k2tog*; repeat from * to * to end of round— 20 (20, 24) sts remain.

**Round 7:** Knit.

**Round 8:** *K3 (3, 4), k2tog*; repeat from * to * to end of round— 16 (16, 20) sts remain.

(continued)

**Round 9:** *K2 (2, 3), k2tog*; repeat from * to * to end of round—
12 (12, 16) sts remain.
**Round 10:** *K1 (1, 2), k2tog*; repeat from * to * to end of round—
8 (8, 12) sts remain.
**Round 11 for size 3 only:** *K1, k2tog*; repeat from * to * to end of round—
8 sts remain. Skip for other sizes.

### FINISHING MAIN PORTION OF MITTEN

Cut yarn leaving a tail at least 8" (20 cm) long. Thread tail onto yarn needle and draw through remaining stitches on needle. Pull to tighten loop and pass yarn needle to inside of mitten and weave yarn tail through stitches to secure.

### MITTEN THUMB

The thumb follows the same stripe pattern as the mitten.

Remove gusset stitches from stitch holder and distribute on three DPNs. Attach yarn B, leaving a tail at least 8" (20 cm) long, and pick up and knit 3 stitches over gap. Place marker to indicate beginning of round, join in the round, and continue to knit as follows:
**Round 1:** Knit until 4 sts remain before end of round, ssk, k1, k2tog (you will need to reposition the BOR marker to fall after the k2tog).
**There should be:** 10 (12, 14) sts.
**Round 2:** Knit.

Repeat round 2 for 8 (9, 9) more rows or until length from beginning of thumb (where stitches were picked up over gusset space) equals 1½" (1¾", 1¾") [4 (4.5, 4.5) cm].

### SHAPE TIP OF THUMB

**Round 1 for size 1:** Knit 8, k2tog—
9 sts remain
**Round 1 for size 2:** Knit.
**Round 1 for size 3:** [K5, k2tog] twice—12 sts remain.
**Round 2:** *K1 (2, 2), k2tog*; repeat from * to * to end of round—
6 (9, 9) sts remain.
**Round 3:** Knit.
**Size 1:** Proceed to directions for finishing thumb.
**Round 4 for sizes 2 and 3:** *K1, k2tog*; repeat from * to * to end of round—
6 sts remain.

### FINISH THUMB

Cut yarn leaving a tail at least 8" (20 cm) long. Thread tail onto yarn needle and draw through remaining stitches on needle. Pull to tighten loop and pass to inside of hat and weave through stitches to secure. Using yarn tail at the base of the thumb, close any gaps that might remain and secure by weaving through stitches.

To finish mittens weave in all other ends and steam lightly.

# Rustic Stripes Hat and Mittens

This hat and mitten set is quick to knit and the combination of sideways rib with reverse stockinette stitch gives the pair a charming, rustic quality. The buttons on the rib band give the knitter an opportunity to add a unique personal touch.

I love to combine self-striping yarns of different colors. I try to choose colors that fight each other a little bit before being combined into a design. If they match too closely then the colors will blend together when knit and lose their distinctive qualities. Three different colors of a thick-and-thin self-striping yarn were used in this design.

## GAUGE

13 sts and 16 rows = 4" (10 cm) in stockinette stitch

*The gauge is the same for both the hat and the mittens.*

## YARN

Bulky weight self-striping yarn

For HAT:

Yarn A: grey tones, 30 yd (27 m)

Yarn B: gold tones, 45 yd (41 m)

Yarn C: pink and purple tones, 25 yd (23 m)

For MITTENS:

Yarn A: grey tones, 36 yd (33 m)

Yarn B: gold tones, 55 yd (50 m)

Yarn C: pink and purple tones, 33 yd (30 m)

Shown: Tahki Yarns *Presto*, 48% wool, 46% acrylic, 3% nylon, 3% mohair; 60 yd (55 m) per 1.75 oz (50 g) ball, Yarn A: color 005 Peppermint, Yarn B: color 002 Curry, and Yarn C: color 003, Cassis.

For HAT or MITTENS: 1 ball of each color.

For both HAT and MITTENS: 2 balls of each color.

## NEEDLES AND NOTIONS

For HAT: US size 10½ (6.5 mm) 16" (41 cm) circular needle or size needed to obtain gauge

For HAT and MITTENS: US size 10½ (6.5 mm) double-point needles or size needed to obtain gauge

US size 9 (5.5 mm) circular needle (or two sizes smaller than size used to obtain gauge). Used only for picking up stitches on band

Optional: US size 10½ (6.5 mm) single-pointed needles or size needed to obtain gauge for making bands.

Optional Magic Loop: circular needle in above sizes at least 40" (100 cm) long for HAT, at least 32" (80 cm) long for MITTENS

Circular stitch markers

Small stitch holder (or waste yarn)

Yarn needle for weaving in ends

1" (2.5 cm) buttons: 2 for HAT, 2 for MITTENS

## RUSTIC STRIPES HAT: Finished Dimensions

| Finished Hat Circumference | Finished Hat Height | Band Width (before edging) |
| --- | --- | --- |
| 22" (56 cm) | 7½" (19 cm) | 3" (7.5 cm) |

## RUSTIC STRIPES HAT

### SIDEWAYS RIB BAND

*A sideways rib band with a buttonhole tab at one end and a button tab at the other is knit first. Stitches are picked up from the finished band and joined in the round to complete the top portion of the hat. All three colors of the yarn are used in both the band and the top section.*

First make the buttonhole tab:

Using larger needle and yarn A, cast on 11 sts.

**Row 1:** Knit.
**Row 2:** Purl.
**Row 3:** K3, yo, K2tog, k1, k2tog, yo, K3.
**Row 4:** Purl.
**Row 5:** Knit.
**Row 6:** P2, p2tog, p3, p2tog, p2—9 sts remain.

### MAIN SECTION

Continue in sideways rib pattern:
**Row 1:** With yarn B, purl.
**Row 2:** With yarn B, knit.
**Row 3:** With yarn B, purl.
**Row 4:** With yarn B, knit.
**Row 5:** With yarn A, purl.
**Row 6:** With yarn A, purl.
**Row 7:** With yarn A, knit.
**Row 8:** With yarn A, purl.

Repeat rows 1–8 eleven more times for a total of twelve repeats.

End by working rows 1–4.

Finish by making the button tab, using yarn A:
**Row 1:** Purl.
**Row 2:** Purl.
**Row 3:** Knit.

**Row 4:** Purl.
**Row 5:** Knit.
**Row 6:** Purl.
**Row 7:** Knit.

Bind off all stitches. (You will be working the bind-off stitches from the purl side but work the bind-off in the traditional way by using knit stitch). The length should be about 24½" (62 cm).

### MAKE EDGING

*A simple edging is added to the sideways rib band to give it a finished look and also to create a foundation for picking up stitches for the top portion of the hat.*

Using #9 (5.5 mm) needle and yarn C, pick up and knit 74 stitches from long edge of band. As a general guide, pick up 5 stitches each in buttonhole tab and button tab and about 5 stitches for every eight-row repeat of the main section.

Knit one row and then bind off all stitches.

Repeat for other edge.

Steam lightly, stretching slightly if necessary. The addition of the edging shortens the length of the band so the final measurement should be about 23½" (59.5 cm).

## TOP SECTION OF HAT

*Stitches are picked up from the edging on the band and joined in the round.*

Position sideways rib band with right side facing, edging running along top and bottom, and button tab at right.

Curl top edge over slightly to view back side of edging bind off row where you will see a string of bumps that look like they form the base of a "V". You will be picking up the stitches for the top of the hat by inserting your needle into these bumps and pulling a loop through to make a stitch.

The smaller #9 (5.5 mm) needle is used to pick up the stitches because the bumps are somewhat tight. Before joining in the round, the stitches are transferred to a larger needle, 16" (40 cm) circular.

Using #9 (5.5 mm) needle and yarn B, pick up 70 stitches from button tab and main section of the band. Do not pick up any stitches from the buttonhole tab portion of the band (1).

2

*The three different colors of yarn in the top portion of the hat can be carried along when not in use by twisting the working yarn around them at the beginning of each round. If preferred, cut the yarn at the end of each stripe and start again when required.*

3

1

Transfer stitches onto #10½ (6.5 mm) 16" (40 cm) circular needle (2) and continue as follows:

Place BOR marker and join in the round, being careful not to twist. Buttonhole tab will be kept free from stitches joined in round (3).

**Round 1:** With yarn B, purl.
**Round 2:** With yarn B, p16, pf&b, p35, pf&b, p17—72 stitches.
**Round 3–4:** With yarn B, purl.
**Round 5:** With yarn A, purl.
**Round 6:** With yarn A, *p6, p2tog*; repeat from * to * to end of round—63 stitches remain.
**Round 7:** With yarn B, purl.
**Round 8:** With yarn B, *p5, p2tog*; repeat from * to * to end of round—54 stitches remain.

(continued)

**Round 9:** With yarn B, purl.
**Round 10:** With yarn C, *p4, p2tog*; repeat from * to * to end of round—45 stitches remain.
**Round 11:** With yarn C, purl.
**Round 12:** *P3, p2tog*; repeat from * to * to end of round with yarn B—36 stitches remain.
**Round 13:** With yarn B, purl.
**Round 14:** *P2, p2tog*; repeat from * to * to end of round with yarn A—27 stitches remain.
**Round 15:** With yarn A, purl.
**Round 16:** *P1, p2tog*; repeat from * to * to end of round with yarn B—18 stitches remain.
**Round 17:** With yarn B, purl.
**Round 18:** *P2tog*; repeat from * to * to end of round with yarn C—9 stitches remain.

**Round 19:** With yarn C, purl.

To finish hat, cut yarn leaving a 10" (25.5 cm) tail. Thread tail onto yarn needle and draw through remaining stitches on needle. Pull to tighten loop and pass to inside of hat and weave through stitches to secure. Weave in all other ends and steam hat lightly.

Overlap buttonhole tab on button tab and mark location for buttons using holes for guide. Attach two buttons as marked.

| RUSTIC STRIPES MITTENS: Finished Dimensions | | |
|---|---|---|
| Circumference at Palm | Finished Length | Band Width (before edging) |
| 8" (20 cm) | 9" (23 cm) | 2¼" (6 cm) |

# RUSTIC STRIPES MITTENS

### SIDEWAYS RIB BAND FOR MITTEN CUFF
Make two alike.

*The cuff is made from a sideways rib band with a buttonhole tab at one end and a button tab at the other. Stitches are picked up from the finished band and joined in the round to complete the main portion of the mitten. All three colors of the yarn are used in both sections.*

First make the buttonhole tab:

Using larger needles and yarn A, cast on 9 stitches:

**Row 1:** Knit.

**Row 2:** Purl.

**Row 3:** K4, yo, k2tog, k3

**Row 4:** Purl.

**Row 5:** Knit.

**Row 6:** P1, p2tog, p3, p2tog, p1— 7 stitches remain.

### MAIN SECTION
Continue in sideways rib pattern:

**Row 1:** With yarn B, purl.

**Row 2:** With yarn B, knit.

**Row 3:** With yarn B, purl.

**Row 4:** With yarn B, knit.

**Row 5:** With yarn A, purl.

**Row 6:** With yarn A, purl.

**Row 7:** With yarn A, knit.

**Row 8:** With yarn A, purl.

Repeat rows 1–8 three more times for a total of four repeats.

End by working just rows 1–4 one time.

Finish by making the button tab, using yarn A:

**Row 1:** Purl.

**Row 2:** Purl.

**Row 3:** Knit.

**Row 4:** Purl.

**Row 5:** Knit.

Bind off all stitches. (You will be working the bind-off stitches from the purl side but work the bind-off in the traditional way using knit stitch). Length from cast-on edge should be approximately 10½" (27 cm).

### MAKE EDGING
*A simple edging is added to the sideways rib band to give it a finished look and also to create a foundation for picking up stitches for the main portion of the mitten.*

Using #9 (5.5 mm) needle and yarn C, pick up and knit 30 stitches along long edge of band. As a general guide, pick up 5 stitches each in button hole tab and button tab and about 5 stitches for every eight-row repeat of the main section.

Knit one row and then bind off all stitches.

Repeat for other edge.

Steam lightly, stretching slightly if necessary. The addition of the edging shortens the length of the band so the final measurement should be about 9½" (24 cm).

### MAIN PORTION OF MITTEN
*Stitches are picked up from the edging and joined in the round. The technique is similar to that used for the hat so please refer to the directions and photos above on page 92 and 93.*

(continued)

## LEFT MITTEN

Position cuff with right side facing and button tab on right edge. Using #9 (5.5 mm) needle and yarn B, pick up 26 stitches from button tab and main section of the band. Do not pick up any stitches from the buttonhole tab portion of the band. Transfer stitches onto #10½ (6.5 mm) DPNs, distribute stitches evenly on four needles.

Join in round being careful not to twist. Buttonhole tab will be kept free from stitches joined in round. With yarn B, purl 13 stitches and place marker to indicate beginning of round.

**Set-up row:** *The beginning of the round is marked on the palm so that color changes can be made in an inconspicuous place.*

*The three different colors of yarn in the main portion of the mitten can be carried along when not in use by twisting the working yarn around them at the beginning of each round. If preferred, cut the yarn at the end of each stripe and start again when required.*

**Round 1:** With yarn B, p7, M1LP, p19.
**Round 2:** With yarn B, p7, pm, M1LP, p1, M1RP, pm, p19—3 sts between markers.
**Round 3:** With yarn A, purl.
**Round 4:** With yarn A, p7, sm, M1LP, p to next marker, M1RP, sm, p19—5 sts between markers.
**Round 5–6:** With yarn B, purl.
**Round 7:** With yarn B, p7, sm, M1LP, p to next marker, M1RP, sm, p19—7 sts between markers.
**Rounds 8–9:** With yarn C, purl.
**Round 10:** With yarn B, p7, sm, M1LP, p to next marker, M1RP, sm, p19—9 sts between markers.
**Round 11:** With yarn B, p7, remove marker, place next 9 sts on holder, remove marker, cast on 1 stitch using backwards thumb loop over gap left by thumb gusset, p19. There should be 27 sts.

**Round 12:** With yarn B, purl.
**Rounds 13–14:** With yarn A, purl.
**Rounds 15–17:** With yarn B, purl.
**Rounds 18–19:** With yarn C, purl.
**Round 20:** With yarn B, p6, p2tog, p19—26 sts remain.
**Round 21:** With yarn B, p6, p2tog, p11, p2tog, p5—24 sts remain.
**Round 22:** With yarn B, *p4, p2tog*; repeat from * to * to end of round—20 sts remain.
**Round 23:** With yarn A, purl.
**Round 24:** With yarn A, *p3, p2tog*; repeat from * to * to end of round—16 sts remain.
**Round 25:** With yarn B, purl.
**Round 26:** With yarn B, *p2, p2tog*; repeat from * to * end of round—12 sts remain.
**Round 27:** With yarn B, *p1, p2tog*; repeat from * to * to end of round—8 sts remain.
**Round 28:** With yarn B, *p2tog*; repeat from * to * to end of round—4 sts remain.

To finish the main portion, cut yarn leaving a 8" (20 cm) tail. Thread tail onto yarn needle and draw through remaining stitches on needle. Pull to tighten loop and pass to inside of mitten and weave through stitches to secure.

## MITTEN THUMB

Remove gusset stitches from stitch holder and distribute on three DPNs. Attach yarn B, leaving a 8" (20 cm) tail, and pick up and knit two stitches over gap. Join in the round and continue to knit as follows:
**Round 1:** With yarn B, p9, p2tog—10 stitches remain.
**Rounds 2–7:** With yarn B, purl.
**Round 8:** With yarn B, p2tog, p1, p2tog, p1, p2tog, p2tog—6 stitches remain.
**Round 9:** With yarn B, purl.

To finish thumb, cut yarn leaving a 8" (20 cm) tail. Thread tail onto yarn needle and draw through remaining stitches on needle. Pull to tighten loop and pass to inside of thumb and weave through stitches to secure. Using yarn tail at the base of the thumb, close any gaps that might remain and secure by weaving through stitches.

## RIGHT MITTEN

Position cuff with right side facing and buttonhole tab on right edge. Skipping the buttonhole tab, use #9 (5.5 mm) needle and yarn B to pick up and knit 26 stitches from the main section of the band and the button tab. Do not pick up any stitches from the buttonhole tab portion of the band. Transfer stitches onto #10½ (6.5 mm) DPNs, distribute stitches evenly on four needles, and continue as follows:

Join in round being careful not to twist. Buttonhole tab will be kept free from stitches joined in round. Purl 13 stitches with yarn B and place marker to indicate beginning of round.

**Set-up row:** *The beginning of the round is marked on the palm so that color changes can be made in an inconspicuous place.*

**Round 1:** With yarn B, p19, M1LP, p7.
**Round 2:** With yarn B, p19, pm, M1LP, p1, M1RP, pm, p7— 3 sts between markers.
**Round 3:** With yarn A, purl.
**Round 4:** With yarn A, p19, sm, M1LP, p to next marker, M1RP, sm, p7— 5 sts between markers.
**Round 5–6:** With yarn B, purl.
**Round 7:** With yarn B, p19, sm, M1LP, p to next marker, M1RP, sm, p7— 7 sts between markers.
**Rounds 8–9:** With yarn C, purl.

**Round 10:** With yarn B, p19, sm, M1LP, p to next marker, M1RP, sm, p7— 9 sts between markers.
**Round 11:** With yarn B, p19, remove marker, place next 9 sts on holder, remove marker, cast on 1 stitch using backwards thumb loop over gap left by thumb gusset, p7. There should be 27 sts.
**Round 12:** With yarn B, purl.
**Rounds 13–14:** With yarn A, purl.
**Rounds 15–17:** With yarn B, purl.
**Rounds 18–19:** With yarn C, purl.
**Round 20:** With yarn B, p18, p2tog, p7—26 sts remain.
**Round 21:** With yarn B, p5, p2tog, p11, p2tog, p6—24 sts remain.
**Round 22:** With yarn B, *p4, p2tog*; repeat from * to * to end of round— 20 sts remain.
**Round 23:** With yarn A, purl.
**Round 24:** With yarn A, *p3, p2tog*; repeat from * to * to end of round— 16 sts remain.
**Round 25:** With yarn B, purl.
**Round 26:** With yarn B, *p2, p2tog*; repeat from * to * end of round— 12 sts remain.
**Round 27:** With yarn B, *p1, p2tog*; repeat from * to * to end of round— 8 sts remain.
**Round 28:** With yarn B, *p2tog*; repeat from * to * to end of round—4 sts remain.

Finish main portion as for left mitten.

Work thumb as for left mitten.

To finish mittens weave in all other ends and steam lightly. Overlap buttonhole tab on button tab and mark location for button using hole for guide. Attach button as marked.

# Stained Glass Hat and Mittens

This slip stitch pattern is a little bit miraculous. At first glance it looks like a complicated stranded knitted design. But it's really just an easy slip stitch pattern made by knitting stripes of bright color between grey bands. At intervals while working the color, two grey stitches are slipped instead of knit. It's those magical stitches that create the stained glass look and also pull the shape of the color blocks into ovals.

Equally as impressive as the stitch pattern is the yarn, which is made from a blend of merino and bamboo that is very soft to the touch and felts like a dream. Who would imagine that it felts so beautifully? The result is wonderfully soft and toasty warm.

The yardage amounts given for the hat are for the large size. Amounts required for the small size are about 15% less, which doesn't change the amount purchased since you still need one ball of each color. If you plan to substitute a different yarn for the hat or mittens, look for a DK weight yarn that is mostly wool (a bit of silk or bamboo is okay). Don't buy a 'superwash' yarn because it won't felt. For best results make a test swatch and measure it before and after it is felted.

## GAUGE

16 sts = 4" (10 cm) in stockinette stitch before felting

20 sts = 4" (10 cm) after felting

Since you will be felting, the yarn is knit at a gauge that is looser than usual for this weight yarn. *The gauge is the same for both the hat and the mittens.*

## YARN

Light weight smooth

For HAT:

Yarn A: grey, 80 yd (73 m)

Yarn B: red, 30 yd (27 m)

Yarn C: green, 35 yd (32 m)

Yarn D: purple, 40 yd (37 m)

Yarn E: teal, 45 yd (41 m)

Shown: Frog Tree Yarns *Meriboo*, 70% merino wool, 30% bamboo; 105 yd (96 m) per 1.75 oz (50 g) ball

Yarn A: #100, 1 ball for HAT, 2 balls for MITTENS

Yarn B: #23, 1 ball for HAT or MITTENS

Yarn C: #46, 1 ball for HAT or MITTENS

Yarn D: #511, 1 ball for HAT or MITTENS

Yarn E: #100, 1 ball for HAT or MITTENS

For both HAT and MITTENS: 3 balls of yarn A and 1 each of the other colors

## NEEDLES AND NOTIONS

For HAT: US size 9 (5.5 mm) 16" (40 cm) circular needle or size required to achieve gauge

For HAT and MITTENS: US size 9 (5 mm) double-pointed needles or size required to achieve gauge

Optional Magic Loop: circular needle in sizes above, at least 40" (101 cm) long for HAT and at least 32" (81 cm) long for MITTENS.

Circular stitch markers

Small stitch holder (or waste yarn)

Yarn needle for weaving in ends

## STAINED GLASS HAT: Size and Finished Dimensions

|  | To Fit Size | Finished Hat Circumference | Finished Hat Height* |
|---|---|---|---|
| **Size 1** | Adult Small | 21" (53 cm) | 7¾" (20 cm) |
| **Size 2** | Adult Medium/Large | 23" (58 cm) | 9" (23 cm) |

*Directions will be shown in the pattern as follows: Size 1 (Size 2)*
*Large size shown on page 98, small size at right*

## STAINED GLASS HAT

*The hat is shaped like a cloche and flares a bit at the bottom. The circumference is measured about 2" (5 cm) from the bottom.*

### CAST ON STITCHES AND BEGIN KNITTING

Using yarn A, cast on 88 (96) stitches. Place BOR marker and join in the round being careful not to twist (see page 20). In the following slip stitch pattern, yarn A is used between each color section (yarns B, C, D, E). Do not cut yarn A between sections; the other colors should be cut leaving a tail at least 8" (20 cm) long for weaving in later.

**Size 1 begins with Round 9.**

**Round 1 for size 2 only:** With yarn A, knit.

**Round 2 for size 2 only:** With yarn A, purl.

**Round 3 for size 2 only:** With yarn B,*sl2, k6*; repeat from * to * to end of round.

**Rounds 4–8, size 2 only:** Repeat round 3.

From this point on the instructions apply to both sizes.

**Round 9:** With yarn A, knit.

**Round 10:** With yarn A, purl.

**Round 11:** With yarn C, k4, *sl2, k6*; repeat from * to * until 4 sts remain, sl2, k2.

**Rounds 12–16:** Repeat round 11.

**Rounds 17–18:** Repeat rounds 9–10.

**Round 19:** With yarn D *sl2, k6*; repeat from * to * to end of round.

**Rounds 20–24:** Repeat round 19.

**Rounds 25–26:** Repeat rounds 9–10.

**Round 27:** With yarn E, k4, *sl2, k6*; repeat from * to * until 4 sts remain, sl2, k2.

**Rounds 28–32:** Repeat round 27.

**Rounds 33–34:** Repeat rounds 9–10.

**Round 35:** With yarn B *sl2, k6*; repeat from * to * to end of round.

**Rounds 36–40:** Repeat round 35.

**Rounds 41–64:** Repeat rounds 9–32.

### SHAPE TOP

Work decreases to shape the crown of the hat. Change to DPNs when the stitches will no longer fit comfortably around the circular needle.

**Rounds 65–66:** Repeat rounds 9–10.

**Rounds 67:** With yarn B, *sl2, k2, k2tog, k2*; repeat from * to * to end of round—77 (84) sts remain.

**Rounds 68–71:** With yarn B, *sl2, k5*; repeat from * to * to end of round.

**Rounds 72–73:** Repeat rounds 9–10.

**Round 74:** With yarn C, k2, *sl2, k1, k2tog, k2*; repeat from * to * until 5 sts remain, sl2, k2tog, k1—66 (72) sts remain.

**Rounds 75–77:** With yarn C, k2, *sl2, k4*; repeat from * to * until 4 sts remain, sl2, k2.

**Rounds 78–79:** Repeat rounds 9–10.

small size

**Round 80:** With yarn D, *sl2, k1, k2tog, k1*; repeat from * to * to end of round—55 (60) sts remain.

**Rounds 81–82:** With yarn D, *sl2, k3*; repeat from * to * to end of round.

**Rounds 83–84:** Repeat rounds 9–10.

**Round 85:** With yarn E, *k2tog, k1, sl2*; repeat from * to * to end of round— 44 (48) sts remain.

**Rounds 86–87:** With yarn E, *k2, sl2*; repeat from * to * to end of round.

**Rounds 88–89:** Repeat rounds 9–10.

**Rounds 90–91:** With yarn B, *sl2, k2*; repeat from * to * to end of round.

**Round 92:** With yarn A, *k2, k2tog*; repeat from * to * to end of round— 33 (36) sts remain.

**Round 93:** With yarn A, knit.

**Round 94:** With yarn A, *k1, k2tog*; repeat from * to * to end of round— 22 (24) sts remain.

**Round 95:** With yarn A, knit.

**Round 96:** With yarn A, *k2tog*; repeat from * to * to end of round— 11 (12) sts remain.

To finish the hat, cut the yarn leaving a tail at least 8" (20 cm) long. Using a yarn needle, thread the tail through the remaining stitches and pass through the hole in the top of the hat to the inside. Pull the tail firmly to close the hole and weave the ends into the stitches on the inside of the hat to secure. Weave in all ends.

See instructions on page 105 for felting.

## STAINED GLASS MITTENS: Finished Dimensions

| Finished Hand Circumference | 7" (18 cm) | |
|---|---|---|
| Finished Mitten Length | 9" (23 cm) | with cuff turned down |
| Finished Mitten Length | 12" (30 cm) | with cuff extended |

# STAINED GLASS MITTENS

*The finished hand circumference can be made smaller or larger when felting. For additional length add extra rows to hand (after gusset is completed) and thumb.*

### CAST ON STITCHES AND BEGIN KNITTING

*Right and left mitten are worked the same for this section.*

Using yarn A, cast on 45 stitches. Place BOR marker and join in the round being careful not to twist (see page 20). In the following slip stitch pattern yarn A is used between each color section (yarns B, C, D, E). Do not cut yarn A between sections; the other colors should be cut leaving a tail at least 8" (20 cm) long for weaving in later.

**Round 1:** With yarn A, knit.
**Round 2:** With yarn A, purl.
**Round 3:** With yarn B, *sl2, k7*; repeat from * to * to end of round.
**Rounds 4–7:** Repeat round 3.
**Round 8:** With yarn B, *sl2, k3, k2tog, k2*; repeat from * to * to end of round— 40 sts remain.
**Round 9:** With yarn A, knit.
**Round 10:** With yarn A, purl.
**Round 11:** With yarn E, k4, *sl2, k6*; repeat from * to * until 4 sts remain, sl2, k2.
**Rounds 12–16:** Repeat round 11.
**Rounds 17–18:** Repeat rounds 9–10.
**Round 19:** With yarn D *sl2, k6*; repeat from * to * to end of round.
**Rounds 20–24:** Repeat round 19.
**Rounds 25–26:** Repeat rounds 9–10.

**Round 27:** With yarn C, k4, *sl2, k6*; repeat from * to * until 4 sts remain, sl2, k2.
**Rounds 28–32:** Repeat round 27.

Change to yarn A for the rest of the mitten.
**Round 33:** *K8, k2tog*; repeat from * to * to end of round—36 sts remain.
**Round 34:** Purl.
**Round 35:** *K1, p1*; repeat from * to * to end of round.

Continue round 35 until length from cast-on row is approximately 8" (20 cm); the ribbing section should be about 4" (10 cm).

### RIGHT MITTEN— MAKE GUSSET FOR THUMB
**Rounds 1–4:** Knit.
**Round 5:** Inc 1, k to end of row—37 sts.
**Round 6:** K9, pm, M1L, k1, M1R, pm, knit to end of round— 3 sts between markers.
**Round 7:** Knit to end of round, slipping markers as you come to them.
**Round 8:** Repeat round 7.
**Round 9:** K9, sm, M1L, k until next marker, M1R, sm, knit to end of round—5 sts between markers.
**Rounds 10–11:** Repeat round 7 twice.
**Round 12:** K9, sm, M1L, k until next marker, M1R, sm, knit to end of round—7 sts between markers.
**Rounds 13–15:** Repeat round 7 three times.
**Round 16:** K9, sm, M1L, k until next marker, M1R, sm, knit to end of round—9 sts between markers.

**Rounds 17–19:**
Repeat round 7 three times.
**Round 20:** K9, sm, M1L, k until next marker, M1R, sm, knit to end of round—11 sts between markers.
**Rounds 21–23:**
Repeat round 7 three times.
**Round 24:** K9, sm, M1L, k until next marker, M1R, sm, knit to end of round—13 sts between markers.
**Round 25:** K9, remove marker, place next 13 sts on holder, remove marker, use backwards thumb loop to cast on 1 st over gap left by gusset stitches, k to end of round.
**Round 26:** Knit.

Repeat round 26 until length from cast-on row is approximately 14½" (37 cm); the stockinette stitch portion should be about 6½" (16.5 cm). If you want to change the length of the mitten add or subtract a few rows from this section.

**SHAPE TIP OF MITTEN**
*Right and left mitten are worked the same for this section.*

Work decreases to shape the tip of the mittens.
**Round 1:** K2tog, k to end of round—36 sts remain.
**Round 2:** *K7, k2tog*; repeat from * to * to end of round—32 sts remain.
**Rounds 3–4:** Knit.
**Round 5:** *K6, k2tog*; repeat from * to * to end of round—28 sts remain.
**Rounds 6–7:** Knit.
**Round 8:** *K5, k2tog*; repeat from * to * to end of round—24 sts remain.
**Round 9:** Knit.
**Round 10:** *K4, k2tog*; repeat from * to * to end of round—20 sts remain.
**Round 11:** Knit.
**Round 12:** *K3, k2tog*; repeat from * to * to end of round—16 sts remain.
**Round 13:** Knit.
**Round 14:** *K2, k2tog*; repeat from * to * to end of round—12 sts remain.
**Round 15:** Knit.

cuff before felting

**Round 16:** *K1, k2tog*; repeat from * to * to end of round—8 sts remain.

**FINISHING MAIN PORTION OF MITTEN**
Please note that the purl side of the mitten is the outside. It is not necessary to pass tail to the inside when weaving in ends—do so on the knit stitch side. Cut yarn leaving a tail at least 8" (20 cm) long. Thread tail onto yarn needle and draw through remaining stitches on needle. Pull to tighten loop and weave yarn tail through stitches to secure.

**LEFT MITTEN—**
**MAKE GUSSET FOR THUMB**
**Rounds 1–4:** Knit.
**Round 5:** Inc 1, k to end of row—37 sts.
**Round 6:** K27, pm, M1L, k1, M1R, pm, knit to end of round—3 sts between markers.
**Rounds 7–8:** Knit to end of round, slipping markers as you come to them.
**Round 9:** K27, sm, M1L, k until next marker, M1R, sm, knit to end of round—5 sts between markers.
**Rounds 10–11:** Repeat rounds 7–8.
**Round 12:** K27, sm, M1L, k until next marker, M1R, sm, knit to end of round—7 sts between markers.

(continued)

**Rounds 13–15:**
Repeat round 7 three times.

**Round 16:** K27, sm, M1L, k until next marker, M1R, sm, knit to end of round—9 sts between markers.

**Rounds 17–19:**
Repeat round 7 three times.

**Round 20:** K27, sm, M1L, k until next marker, M1R, sm, knit to end of round—11 sts between markers.

**Rounds 21–23:**
Repeat round 7 three times.

**Round 24:** K27, sm, M1L, k until next marker, M1R, sm, knit to end of round—13 sts between markers.

**Round 25:** K27, remove marker, place next 13 sts on holder, remove marker, use backwards thumb loop to cast on 1 st over gap left by gusset stitches, k to end of round.

**Round 26:** Knit.

Repeat round 26 until length from cast-on row is approximately 14½" (37 cm). The stockinette stitch portion should be about 6½" (16.5 cm). If you want to change the length of the mitten add or subtract a few rows from this section.

To finish main portion of left mitten refer Shape Tip of Mitten (page 103).

## MITTEN THUMB

*Right and left mittens are worked the same for this section.*

Remove gusset stitches from stitch holder and distribute on three DPNs. Attach yarn B, leaving a tail at least 8" (20 cm) long and pick up and knit 2 stitches over gap. Join in the round and continue to knit as follows:

**Round 1:** K13, k2 tog, pm to indicate beginning of round—14 sts remain.

Repeat round 1 until length from beginning of thumb (where stitches were picked up over gusset space) equals 2½" (6.5 cm).

### SHAPE TIP OF THUMB

**Round 1:** [K5, k2tog] twice—12 sts remain.
**Round 2:** *K2, k2tog*; repeat from * to * to end of round—9 sts remain.
**Rounds 3–4:** Knit.
**Round 5:** *K1, k2tog*; repeat from * to * to end of round—6 sts remain.

### FINISH THUMB

It is not necessary to pass tail to the inside when weaving in ends—do so on the knit stitch side. Cut yarn leaving a tail at least 8" (20 cm) long. Thread tail onto yarn needle and draw through remaining stitches on needle. Pull to tighten loop and weave through stitches to secure. Using yarn tail at the base of the thumb, close any gaps that might remain and secure by weaving through stitches. Weave in all other ends and turn mitten right side out so the purl side is showing.

### FELTING HAT AND MITTENS

Before felting, turn mittens right side out so that the purl side is showing. If you are using the merino and bamboo yarn specified in this pattern then please be aware that it felts very quickly! In my washer (a top loader) the items felted in five minutes using warm water. If you have substituted a different yarn, it is a good idea to felt a test swatch first to understand how much the stitches will shrink and how long the process will take.

The felting process requires three elements: agitation, soap, and heat. Agitation comes from your washer set to the lowest water level. Also, put in some old jeans or tennis shoes or any other lint-free washable item to help bash your knitting around. A little bit of soap is essential. I use a special wool wash soap that doesn't need to be rinsed so I don't have to worry about too many suds. You need warm, not hot, water to felt the merino bamboo blend. If you are using 100% wool, then you may need hot water.

The hardest part of felting is putting your knitted "baby" into the washer for the first time. Go ahead and throw it in—low water level, extra items to help with agitation, a bit of soap, and warm water. Then don't go anywhere! After two minutes remove items to check for fit and felting. The stitches will begin to become less distinct and eventually the surface will assume an all-over bumpy texture depending on how much you choose to felt your item. You will be able to adjust the size to a certain degree by how much you allow the hat and mittens to felt. Stop the washer after just a few minutes and remove the item. Squeeze out the excess water and check the size. If it's still too big then return it to the washer for some more felting. If the size seems right then stop felting. Every time you pull an item out of the washer to check for fit, pull it from side to side as necessary to encourage it to assume its final shape, even if it's too big at this point.

Remove and rinse in cool water in the sink. Wrap in towels to remove excess moisture, pull from side to side as necessary to establish correct shape, and then lay flat to dry. Don't spin your items dry in the washer as this could cause permanent creases.

# Color Therapy
# Slip Stitch Hat and Mittens

This hat pattern has been a staple in my shop for years, and coming up with different color combinations is like therapy for me. I love the interplay of color in the slip stitch pattern and it's a great way to use up leftover yarn. I recently designed the mitten pattern to match and it has already become a big hit.

I adore lots of color and I always find myself drawn to what I call semi-solid hand-dyed yarns. These are subtly variegated and the color seems more like a watercolor wash than a solid dye. Since each color contains undertones of several other colors, the combinations can be incredibly beautiful. In addition, I have to say that my favorite fiber is merino. I enjoy working with this springy yarn. It has a beautiful hand when finished and its memory is forgiving to even the beginning knitters among us.

All of the designs use five different colors in approximately equal amounts. If you want the top of the hat to be a solid color as shown in the man's hat (size 4) then about 30% of the yarn should be in that color with the remainder equally divided between the other four colors. If you plan to use a different number of colors, keep in mind that an odd number is best. If you are making both the hat and the mittens then one skein of each color is more than enough (in fact you will be able to make a few sets).

*For best results make a gauge of the slip stitch pattern in the round; try casting on 40 stitches (any even number will do). If you prefer to make a swatch that is knit flat, see the Slip Stitch Pattern in Rows, page 108.*

man's hat

woman's hat

child's hat

## GAUGE

20 sts = 4" (10 cm) in stockinette stitch

22 sts = 4" (10 cm) in slip stitch pattern

*The gauge is the same for both the hat and the mittens.*

## YARN

Medium weight smooth yarn; the total yardage required for each size is shown in the charts.

Shown: Dream in Color *Classy,* 100% merino wool; 250 yd (228 m) per 4 oz (112 g) skein.

Size 1 colors: Lipstick Lava, Visual Purple, Happy Forest, Gold Experience, Blue Lagoon

Size 3 colors: Midnight Derby, Go Go Grassy, Ruby River, Pansy Go Lightly, Lunar Zazzle

Size 4 colors: November Muse, Spring Tickle, Night Watch, Strange Harvest, Shiny Moss

## NEEDLES AND NOTIONS

For HAT: US size 7 (4.5 mm) 16" (40 cm) circular needle or size required to achieve gauge

For HAT and MITTENS: US size 7 (4.5 mm) double-pointed needles or size required to achieve gauge

For MITTENS: US size 5 (3.75 mm) double-pointed needles (or two sizes smaller than size used to achieve gauge)

Optional Magic Loop: circular needle in sizes above, at least 40" (101 cm) long for HAT and at least 32" (81 cm) long for MITTENS.

Circular stitch markers

Small stitch holder (or waste yarn)

Yarn needle for weaving in ends

## ABBREVIATIONS

SSP = slip stitch pattern (page 108)

For all other abbreviations see page 144.

### SLIP STITCH PATTERN (SSP)

Note that exact colors aren't specified. You can follow the color pattern shown in the photos or make up your own. Also, it isn't important to follow the same color pattern throughout—sometimes a "mistake" can be better than the original plan. Rather than cut the colors between rounds, bring the unused yarn along with you! When you reach the last stitch of round 1 of the SSP, pass the working yarn under the other strands before working the stitch. This will make a loop around the "bundle" of other colored yarns and bring them along as work progresses.

**Round 1:** Change color, knit.
**Round 2:** Purl.
**Round 3:** Change color, *knit 1, slip 1*, repeat from * to * until the end of the round.
**Round 4:** *Purl 1, wyib slip 1*, repeat from * to * until the end of the round.

    Repeat Rounds 1 to 4 until desired length.

### SSP IN ROWS

If you are making a swatch that is knit flat (working back and forth instead of in the round) then work the rows as follows:

**Row 1:** Change color, knit.
**Row 2:** Knit.
**Row 3:** Change color, *knit 1, slip 1*, repeat from * to * until the end of the row.
**Row 4:** *K1, wyif slip 1*, repeat from * to * until the end of the row.

Repeat Rows 1 to 4 until desired length.

### STRIPE PATTERN

While following the slip stitch pattern (a four-round repeat), the color is changed every other round. In other words, each color is used for two rounds before changing to a new color. This design looks best when five colors are repeated in sequence. If you plan to use a different number of colors, keep in mind that an odd number of colors is best.

## COLOR THERAPY SLIP STITCH HAT: Size, Finished Dimensions, and Yardage

| | To Fit Size | Finished Hat Circumference | Short Hat Height | Tall Hat Height | Approximate Yardage Required |
|---|---|---|---|---|---|
| Size 1 | 2 to 4 year | 18" (46 cm) | 6¾" (17 cm) | 7½" (19 cm) | 140 to 155 yd (128 to 140 m) |
| Size 2 | 5 year to Adult Small | 19" (48 cm) | 7¼" (18 cm) | 8½" (22 cm) | 165 to 180 yd (151 to 160 m) |
| Size 3 | Adult Medium | 20½" (52 cm) | 8¼" (21 cm) | 9" (23 cm) | 185 to 200 yd (169 to 183 m) |
| Size 4 | Adult Large | 22½" (57 cm) | 8¾" (22 cm) | 9¾" (25 cm) | 200 to 220 yd (183 to 201 m) |

*Directions will be shown in the pattern as follows: Size 1 (Size 2, Size 3, Size 4)*

## COLOR THERAPY SLIP STITCH HAT

*The short version fits like a skull cap and the tall version will stand slightly above the average head.*

**CAST ON STITCHES AND BEGIN KNITTING**
Using circular needle, cast on 100 (104, 112, 124) stitches. Place

BOR marker and join in the round being careful not to twist (see page 20).

Work two rounds in ribbing as follows:

**Round 1:** *K2, p2*; repeat from * to * until the end of the round.

**Round 2:** Repeat round 1.

*At this point you will change to a new color and begin the SSP. Remember that the stitch pattern is repeated every four rounds and the color is changed every two rounds. Note that round 3 for size 2 is different since a few stitches need to be increased just this once.*

**Round 3 for size 1, 3, and 4:** SSP Round 1 to end of round.

**Round 3 for size 2:** While working SSP Round 1, [k51, kf&b]twice—106 sts.

**Round 4:** SSP Round 2 to end of round.

**Round 5:** SSP Round 3 to end of round.

**Round 6:** SSP Round 4 to end of round.

Continue to repeat the SSP rounds as established above until the beginning of the decrease section to shape the top of the hat.

## SHAPE TOP

Work decreases to shape the hat crown. Discontinue the SSP after SSP Round 4 is completed and the length from the cast-on edge is:

4¼" (4¾", 5½" 6") [11 (12, 14, 18) cm] for short hat

5" (5¾", 6¼" 7") [12.5 (14.5, 16, 18) cm] for tall hat

Make the length from the cast-on edge a bit shorter or longer in order to complete the SSP through round 4.

Stop the SSP at this point and work in stockinette stitch (all knit) and at the same time change colors every four rows. If preferred the top section can be made all in one color or any stripe sequence you prefer. Change to DPNs when the stitches will no longer fit comfortably around the circular needle. Each size has unique directions for the first three rounds; after that the directions are the same for all sizes.

### SIZE 1

**Round 1:** Change color, knit.

**Round 2:** *K8, k2tog*, repeat from * to * to end of round—90 sts remain.

**Round 3:** Knit.

### SIZE 2

**Round 1:** Change color, knit.

**Round 2:** [K8, k2tog] 10 times, k6—96 sts remain.

**Round 3:** *Knit 14, k2tog*; repeat from * to * to end of round—90 sts remain.

### SIZE 3

**Round 1:** Change color, knit.

**Round 2:** [K8, k2tog] 11 times, k2—102 sts remain.

**Round 3:** Knit 49, k2tog, k to end of round—100 sts remain.

### SIZE 4

**Round 1:** Change color, knit.

**Round 2:** [K8, k2tog] 12 times, k4—112 sts remain.

**Round 3:** [K54, k2tog] twice—110 sts remain.

### ALL SIZES

**Round 4:** *K8, k2tog*; repeat from * to * to end of round—81 (81, 90, 99) sts remain.

**Round 5:** Change color, knit.

**Round 6:** *K7, k2tog*; repeat from * to * to end of round—72 (72, 80, 88) sts remain.

**Round 7:** Knit.

**Round 8:** *K6, k2tog*; repeat from * to * to end of round—63 (63, 70, 77) sts remain.

**Round 9:** Change color, knit.

**Round 10:** *K5, k2tog*; repeat from * to * to end of round—54 (54, 60, 66) sts remain.

**Round 11:** Knit.

**Round 12:** *K4, k2tog*; repeat from * to * to end of round—45 (45, 50, 55) sts remain.

**Round 13:** Change color, knit.

(continued)

**Round 14:** *K3, k2tog*; repeat from
* to * to end of round—
36 (36, 40, 44) sts remain.
**Round 15:** Knit.
**Round 16:** *K2, k2tog*; repeat from
* to * to end of round—
27 (27, 30, 33) sts remain.
**Round 17:** Change color, knit.
**Round 18:** *K1, k2tog*; repeat from
* to * to end of round—
18 (18, 20, 22) sts remain.
**Round 19:** Knit.
**Round 20:** *K2tog*; repeat from * to *
to end of round—9 (9, 10, 11) sts remain.
**Round 21:** Change color, knit.
**Round 22 for sizes 1 and 2:** *K2tog*;
repeat from * to * until 1 st remains,
k1—5 sts remain.
**Round 22 for size 3:** *K2tog*; repeat
from * to * to end of round—5 sts remain.
**Round 22 for size 4:** *K2tog*; repeat
from * to * until 1 st remains, k1—
6 sts remain.

If making optional I-cord knot,
continue with row 23 as follows:
**Round 23 for sizes 1, 2, and 3:** K2tog,
k to end of round—4 sts remain.
**Round 23 for size 4:** [K2tog] twice, k to
end of round—4 sts remain.

### OPTIONAL I-CORD KNOT
See page 65 for directions.

### PLAIN TOP WITHOUT I-CORD KNOT
After round 22 is completed, cut the
yarn leaving a tail at least 8" (20 cm)
long. Using a yarn needle, thread the tail
through the remaining stitches and pass
through the hole in the top of the hat to
the inside. Pull the tail firmly to close the
hole and weave the ends into the stitches
on the inside of the hat to secure.

To finish hat, weave in all other ends
and steam lightly.

| | To Fit Size | Finished Hat Circumference | Finished Length | Approximate Yardage Required |
|---|---|---|---|---|
| **Size 1** | 2 to 4 year | 5½" (14 cm) | 5½" (14 cm) | 40 yd (37 m) |
| **Size 2** | 5 to 9 year | 6¼" (16 cm) | 6½" (17 cm) | 55 yd (50 m) |
| **Size 3** | 10 year to Women's Small | 7¼" (18 cm) | 7¾" (20 cm) | 70 yd (64 m) |
| **Size 4** | Women's Med./ Large | 7½" (19 cm) | 9" (23 cm) | 85 yd (78 m) |
| **Size 5** | Men's Med./ Large | 8½" (22 cm) | 10½" (27 cm) | 100 yd (91 m) |

**COLOR THERAPY SLIP STITCH MITTENS: Size, Finished Dimensions, and Yardage**

*Directions will be shown in the pattern as follows: Size 1 (Size 2, Size 3, Size 4, Size 5)*

## COLOR THERAPY SLIP STITCH MITTENS

*When working from a pattern with a large number of sizes it's a good idea to photocopy the pattern before you start and highlight all the directions applying to the size you are making.*

### CAST ON STITCHES
### AND MAKE RIBBED CUFF

Right and left mittens are worked the same for this section.

Using smaller needles, cast on 28 (32, 36, 40, 44) sts. Place BOR marker and join in the round being careful not to twist (see page 20).

**Round 1:** *K2, p2*; repeat from * to * to end of round.

Repeat round 1 until cuff measures 1½" (1¾", 1¾", 2", 2½") [4 (4.5, 4.5, 5, 6.5) cm].

Change to larger needles and **knit one round.**

*At this point you will change to a new color and begin the SSP. Remember that the stitch pattern is repeated every four rows and the color is changed every two rows. The gusset directions are different for the right and left mitten. Directions for left mitten gusset begin on page 115.*

### RIGHT MITTEN—
### MAKE GUSSET FOR THUMB

**Round 1:** SSP Round 1 for 18, (21, 24, 27, 30) sts, k4, SSP Round 1 to end of round.

**Round 2:** SSP Round 2 for 18, (21, 24, 27, 30) sts, k4, SSP Round 2 to end of round.

**Round 3:** SSP Round 3 for 18, (21, 24, 27, 30) sts, k4, SSP Round 3 to end of round.

**Round 4:** SSP Round 4 for 18, (21, 24, 27, 30) sts, k2, inc1, k2, SSP Round 4 to end of round.

Continue to repeat the SSP rounds as established above until decrease section for the mitten tip.

**Round 5:** SSP for 18 (21, 24, 27, 30) sts, pm, k5, pm, SSP to end of round— 5 sts between markers.

**Round 6:** SSP for 18 (21, 24, 27, 30) sts, sm, k2, M1R, k1, M1L, k2, sm, SSP to end of round—7 sts between markers.

**Round 7:** SSP for 18 (21, 24, 27, 30) sts, sm, knit to next marker, sm, SSP to end of round.

(continued)

**Round 8 for size 1 only:** SSP for 18 sts, sm, knit to next marker, sm, SSP to end of round. Skip for other sizes.

**Round 9:** SSP for 18 (21, 24, 27, 30) sts, sm, k3, M1R, k1, M1L, k3, sm, SSP to end of round—9 sts between markers.

**Round 10:** SSP for 18 (21, 24, 27, 30) sts, sm, knit to next marker, sm, SSP to end of round.

**Round 11 for sizes 1 and 2 only:** SSP for 18 (21, -, -, -, -) sts, sm, knit to next marker, sm, SSP to end of round. Skip for other sizes.

**Round 12:** SSP for 18 (21, 24, 27, 30) sts, sm, k4, M1R, k1, M1L, k4, sm, SSP to end of round—11 sts between markers.

**Round 13:** SSP for 18 (21, 24, 27, 30) sts, sm, knit to next marker, sm, SSP to end of round.

**Round 14 for sizes 1, 2, and 3 only:** SSP for 18 (21, 24, -, -) sts, sm, knit to next marker, sm, SSP to end of round. Skip for other sizes.

**Round 15:** SSP for 18 (21, 24, 27, 30) sts, sm, k5, M1R, k1, M1L, k5, sm, SSP to end of round—13 sts between markers.

**Round 16:** SSP for 18 (21, 24, 27, 30) sts, sm, knit to next marker, sm, SSP to end of round.

**Size 1: Proceed to round 29.**

**Round 17 for sizes 2, 3, and 4 only:** SSP for - (21, 24, 27, -) sts, sm, knit to next marker, sm, SSP to end of round. Skip for other sizes.

**Round 18 for sizes 2, 3, 4, and 5 only:** SSP for - (21, 24, 27, 30) sts, sm, k6, M1R, k1, M1L, k6, sm, SSP to end of round—15 sts between markers.

**Round 19 for sizes 2, 3, 4, and 5 only:** SSP for - (21, 24, 27, 30) sts, sm, knit to next marker, sm, SSP to end of round.

**Size 2: Proceed to round 29.**

**Round 20 for sizes 3, 4, and 5 only:** SSP for - (-, 24, 27, 30) sts, sm, knit to next marker, sm, SSP to end of round.

**Round 21 for sizes 3, 4, and 5 only:** SSP for - (-, 24, 27, 30) sts, sm, k7, M1R, k1, M1L, k7, sm, SSP to end of round—17 sts between markers.

**Round 22 for sizes 3, 4, and 5 only:** SSP for - (-, 24, 27, 30) sts, sm, knit to next marker, sm, SSP to end of round.

**Size 3: Proceed to round 29.**

**Round 23 for sizes 4 and 5 only:** SSP for - (-, -, 27, 30) sts, sm, knit to next marker, sm, SSP to end of round.

**Round 24 for sizes 4 and 5 only:** SSP for - (-, -, 27, 30) sts, sm, k8, M1R, k1, M1L, k8, sm, SSP to end of round—19 sts between markers.

**Round 25 for sizes 4 and 5 only:** SSP for - (-, -, 27, 30) sts, sm, knit to next marker, sm, SSP to end of round.

**Size 4: Proceed to round 29.**

**Round 26 for size 5 only:** SSP for 30 sts, sm, knit to next marker, sm, SSP to end of round.

**Round 27 for size 5 only:** SSP for 30 sts, sm, k9, M1R, k1, M1L, k9, sm, SSP to end of round—21 sts between markers.

**Round 28 for size 5 only:** SSP for 30 sts, sm, knit to next marker, sm, SSP to end of round.

**Round 29:** SSP to marker, remove marker, k2, place next 9 (11, 13, 15, 17) sts on holder, remove marker, use backwards thumb loop to cast on 1 st over gap left by gusset stitches, k2, SSP to end of round.

**Round 30:** SSP for 18, (21, 24, 27, 30) sts, k5, SSP to end of round.

Continue previous round, if necessary, until you have completed round 4 of SSP.

**Next round (Round 1 of SSP):** K18 (21, 24, 27, 30) sts, k1, k2tog, k2, SSP to end of round—28 (32, 36, 40, 44) sts remain.

**Next round (Round 2 of SSP):** Purl all sts to end of round.

Continue working SSP on **all** sts until length from cast-on round is approximately 4½" (5¼", 6¼", 7¼", 8¼") [11.5 (13.5, 16, 18.5, 21) cm] **AND** you have just completed Round 4 of the SSP. Make the length from the cuff a bit shorter or longer in order to complete the SSP through Round 4.

## SHAPE TIP OF MITTEN

Right and left mittens are worked the same for this section.

Work decreases to shape the tip of the mittens.

Discontinue SSP at this point and knit all sts working decreases as shown below. You can continue changing the color every two rows or change to a different striping sequence (for instance, every four rows) or use just one color.

**Round 1:** *Knit 5 (6,7, 8, 9) sts, k2tog*; repeat from * to * to end of round—24 (28, 32, 36, 40) sts remain.

**Round 2:** Knit.

**Round 3:** *Knit 4 (5, 6, 7, 8) sts, k2tog*; repeat from * to * to end of round—20 (24, 28, 32, 36) sts remain.

**Round 4:** Knit.

**Round 5:** *Knit 3 (4, 5, 6, 7) sts, k2tog*; repeat from * to * to end of round—16 (20, 24, 28, 32) sts remain.

**Round 6, size 2, 3, 4, and 5 only:** Knit. Skip for other sizes.

**Round 7:** *Knit 2 (3, 4, 5, 6) sts, k2tog*; repeat from * to * to end of round—12 (16, 20, 24, 28) sts remain.

**Round 8 for sizes 4 and 5 only:** Knit. Skip for other sizes.

**Round 9:** *Knit 1 (2, 3, 4, 5) sts, k2tog*; repeat from * to * to end of round—8 (12, 16, 20, 24) sts remain.

**Size 1: Proceed to round 14.**

**Round 10 for sizes 2, 3, 4, and 5 only:** *Knit - (1, 2, 3, 4) sts, k2tog*; repeat from * to * to end of round—- (8, 12, 16, 20) sts remain.

**Size 2: Proceed to round 14.**

**Round 11 for sizes 3, 4, and 5 only:** *Knit - (-, 1, 2, 3) sts, k2tog*; repeat from * to * to end of round—- (-, 8, 12, 16) sts remain.

**Size 3: Proceed to round 14.**

**Round 12 for sizes 4 and 5 only:** *Knit - (-, -, 1, 2) sts, k2tog*; repeat from * to * to end of round—- (-, -, 8, 12) sts remain.

**Size 4: Proceed to directions for Finishing Main Portion of Mitten.**

(continued)

**Round 13 for size 5 only:** *K1, k2tog*; repeat from * to * to end of round—8 sts remain.

**Size 5:** Proceed to directions for Finishing Main Portion of Mitten.

**Round 14 for sizes 1, 2, and 3 only:** *K2tog*; repeat from * to * to end of round—4 sts remain.

### FINISHING MAIN PORTION OF MITTEN

Cut yarn leaving a tail at least 8" (20 cm) long. Thread tail onto yarn needle and draw through remaining stitches on needle. Pull to tighten loop and pass yarn needle to inside of mitten and weave yarn tail through stitches to secure.

### MITTEN THUMB

Right and left mittens are worked the same for this section.

Discontinue SSP and work all thumb sts in knit stitch. The thumb can be knit all in one color or a few different colors. Don't change the stripe colors too frequently on the thumb; it gets crowded in there and lots of yarn ends can complicate the knitting!

Remove gusset stitches from stitch holder and distribute on three DPNs. Attach yarn leaving an 8" (20 cm) tail, pick up and knit 2 (2, 2, 4, 4) stitches over gap.

Place marker to indicate beginning of round, join in the round and continue to knit as follows:

**Round 1 for sizes 1, 2, and 3:** Knit until 2 sts remain before end of round, k2tog.

**Round 1 for sizes 4 and 5:** Knit until 4 sts remain before end of round, [k2tog] twice.

You should have 10 (12, 14, 17, 19) sts.

**Round 2:** Knit

Repeat round 2 for 5 (7, 7, 9, 9) more rounds or until length from beginning of thumb (where stitches were picked up over gusset space) equals ¾" (1", 1", 1¼", 1¼") [2 (2.5, 2.5, 3, 3) cm].

### SHAPE TIP OF THUMB

#### SIZE 1

**Round 1:** Knit 8, k2tog—9 sts remain.

**Round 2:** [K1, k2tog] three times—6 sts remain.

**Round 3:** Knit.

Proceed to directions for finishing thumb.

#### SIZES 2 AND 3

**Round 1 for size 3 only:** [K5, 2tog] twice—12 sts remain.

**Round 2:** [K2, k2tog] three times—9 sts remain.

**Round 3:** Knit.

**Round 4:** [K1, k2tog] three times—6 sts remain.

Proceed to directions for finishing thumb.

#### SIZE 4

**Round 1:** Knit 6, k2tog, k7, k2tog—15 sts remain.

**Round 2:** [K3, k2tog] three times—12 sts remain

**Round 3:** Knit.

**Round 4:** [K2, k2tog] three times—9 sts remain.

**Round 5:** [K1, k2tog] three times—6 sts remain.

Proceed to directions for finishing thumb.

#### SIZE 5

**Round 1:** Knit 8, k2tog, k9—18 sts remain.

**Round 2:** [Knit 4, k2tog] three times—15 sts remain.

**Round 3:** Knit.

**Round 4:** [K3, k2tog] three times—12 sts remain.

**Round 5:** Knit.

**Round 6:** [K2, k2tog] three times—9 sts remain.

**Round 7:** [K1, k2tog] three times—6 sts remain.

Proceed to directions for finishing thumb.

## FINISH THUMB

Cut yarn leaving a tail at least 8" (20 cm) long. Thread tail onto yarn needle and draw through remaining stitches on needle. Pull to tighten loop and pass to inside of hat and weave through stitches to secure. Using yarn tail at the base of the thumb, close any gaps that might remain and secure by weaving through stitches.

## LEFT MITTEN— MAKE GUSSET FOR THUMB

**Round 1:** SSP Round 1 for 6 (7, 8, 9, 10) sts, k4, SSP Round 1 to end of round.

**Round 2:** SSP Round 2 for 6 (7, 8, 9, 10) sts, k4, SSP Round 2 to end of round.

**Round 3:** SSP Round 3 for 6 (7, 8, 9, 10) sts, k4, SSP Round 3 to end of round.

**Round 4:** SSP Round 4 for 6 (7, 8, 9, 10) sts, k2, inc1, k2, SSP Round 4 to end of round.

Continue to repeat the SSP rounds as established above until decrease section for the mitten tip.

**Round 5:** SSP for 6 (7, 8, 9, 10) sts, pm, k5, pm, SSP to end of round— 5 sts between markers.

**Round 6:** SSP for 6 (7, 8, 9, 10) sts, sm, k2, M1R, k1, M1L, k2, sm, SSP to end of round—7 sts between markers.

**Round 7:** SSP for 6 (7, 8, 9, 10) sts, sm, knit to next marker, sm, SSP to end of round.

**Round 8 for size 1 only:** SSP for 6 sts, sm, knit to next marker, sm, SSP to end of round. Skip for other sizes.

**Round 9:** SSP for 6 (7, 8, 9, 10) sts, sm, k3, M1R, k1, M1L, k3, sm, SSP to end of round—9 sts between markers.

**Round 10:** SSP for 6 (7, 8, 9, 10) sts, sm, knit to next marker, sm, SSP to end of round.

**Round 11 for sizes 1 and 2 only:** SSP for 6 (7, -, -, -) sts, sm, knit to next marker, sm, SSP to end of round. Skip for other sizes.

**Round 12:** SSP for 6 (7, 8, 9, 10) sts, sm, k4, M1R, k1, M1L, k4, sm, SSP to end of round—11 sts between markers.

**Round 13:** SSP for 6 (7, 8, 9, 10) sts, sm, knit to next marker, sm, SSP to end of round.

**Round 14 for sizes 1, 2, and 3 only:** SSP for 6 (7, 8, -, -) sts, sm, knit to next marker, sm, SSP to end of round. Skip for other sizes.

**Round 15:** SSP for 6 (7, 8, 9, 10) sts, sm, k5, M1R, k1, M1L, k5, sm, SSP to end of round—13 sts between markers.

*(continued)*

**Round 16:** SSP for 6 (7, 8, 9, 10) sts, sm, knit to next marker, sm, SSP to end of round.

**Size 1: Proceed to round 29.**

**Round 17 for sizes 2, 3, and 4 only:** SSP for - (6, 7, 8, -) sts, sm, knit to next marker, sm, SSP to end of round.

**Round 18 for sizes 2, 3, 4, and 5 only:** SSP for - (7, 8, 9, 10) sts, sm, k6, M1R, k1, M1L, k6, sm, SSP to end of round—15 sts between markers.

**Round 19 for sizes 2, 3, 4, and 5 only:** SSP for - (7, 8, 9, 10) sts, sm, knit to next marker, sm, SSP to end of round.

**Size 2: Proceed to round 29.**

**Round 20 for sizes 3, 4, and 5 only:** SSP for - (-, 8, 9, 10) sts, sm, knit to next marker, sm, SSP to end of round.

**Round 21 for sizes 3, 4, and 5 only:** SSP for - (-, 8, 9, 10) sts, sm, k7, M1R, k1, M1L, k7, sm, SSP to end of round—17 sts between markers.

**Round 22 for sizes 3, 4, and 5 only:** SSP for - (-, 8, 9, 10) sts, sm, knit to next marker, sm, SSP to end of round.

**Size 3: Proceed to round 29.**

**Round 23 for sizes 4 and 5 only:** SSP for - (-, -, 9, 10) sts, sm, knit to next marker, sm, SSP to end of round.

**Round 24 for sizes 4 and 5 only:** SSP for - (-, -, 9, 10) sts, sm, k8, M1R, k1, M1L, k8, sm, SSP to end of round— 19 sts between markers.

**Round 25 for sizes 4 and 5 only:** SSP for - (-, -, 9, 10) sts, sm, knit to next marker, sm, SSP to end of round.

**Size 4: Proceed to round 29.**

**Round 26 for size 5 only:** SSP for 10 sts, sm, knit to next marker, sm, SSP to end of round.

**Round 27 for size 5 only:** SSP for 10 sts, sm, k9, M1R, k1, M1L, k9, sm, SSP to end of round—21 sts between markers.

**Round 28 for size 5 only:** SSP for 10 sts, sm, knit to next marker, sm, SSP to end of round.

**Round 29:** SSP to marker, remove marker, k2, place next 9 (11, 13, 15, 17) sts on holder, remove marker, use backwards thumb loop to cast on 1 st over gap left by gusset stitches, k2, SSP to end of round.

**Round 30:** SSP for 6 (7, 8, 9, 10) sts, k5, SSP to end of round.

Continue previous round, if necessary, until you have completed Round 4 of SSP.

**Next round (Round 1 of SSP):** 6 (7, 8, 9, 10) sts, k1, k2tog, k2, SSP to end of round—28 (32, 36, 40, 44) sts remain.

**Next round (Round 2 of SSP):** Purl all sts to end of round.

Continue working SSP on **all** sts until length from cast-on round is approximately 4½" (5¼", 6¼", 7¼", 8¼") [11.5 (13.5, 16, 18.5, 21) cm] **AND** you have just completed Round 4 of the SSP. Make the length from the cuff a bit shorter or longer in order to complete the SSP through Round 4.

Finish main portion as for right mitten, see directions for Shape Tip of Mitten on page 113.

Work thumb as for right mitten, see directions page 114.

To finish mittens, weave in all other ends and steam lightly.

# Berry Stitch Hat and Mittens for Men

All too often men's hats and mittens lack creativity and excitement compared to women's. For this design, I have used a stitch that engages the knitter and imparts artistry while still keeping the flavor masculine.

The design combines two yarns, a simple solid colored merino and a hand-dyed sock-weight yarn that is double stranded. The hat and mittens will fit an average adult male but the size can easily be adjusted.

The berry stitch pattern for the hat is a multiple of four stitches. If you would like to make the hat larger or smaller, add or subtract to the number of cast-on stitches in a multiple of four. For instance for a smaller hat, cast on 112 stitches or for a larger hat cast on 124 or 128 stitches. You will also need to change the length appropriately.

## GAUGE

For HAT: 22 sts and 28 rows = 4" (10 cm) in k3, p1 ribbing

For MITTENS: 24 sts and 28 rows = 4" (10 cm) in k3, p1 ribbing

## YARN

Yarn A: Super fine weight smooth yarn, HAT: 100 yd (91 m); MITTENS: 130 yd (119 m)

Shown: Dream in Color *Knitosophy*, 100% merino wool; 450 yd (411 m) per 4 oz (112 g) skein, color Superhero, HAT: 1 skein, MITTENS: 1 skein

*To substitute a heavier yarn for yarn A that does not need to be doubled, choose a DK weight yarn similar to yarn B.*

Yarn B: Light weight smooth yarn, HAT: 130 yd (119 m); MITTENS: 130 yd (119 m)

Shown: Debbie Bliss *Rialto* DK, 100% merino wool; 105 yd (96 m) per 1.75 oz (50 g) ball, color #010; HAT: 2 balls, MITTENS: 2 balls

*To make both the hat and the mittens: 1 skein of yarn A and 3 balls of yarn B.*

## NEEDLES AND NOTIONS

For HAT:

US size 7 (4.5 mm) 16" (40 cm) circular needle or size needed to achieve gauge

US size 6 (4 mm) 16" (40 cm) circular needle (or one size smaller than size needed to achieve gauge)

US size 7 (4.5 mm) double-pointed needles or size needed to achieve gauge

For MITTENS:

US size 6 (4 mm) double-pointed needles or size needed to achieve gauge

US size 5 (3.75 mm) double-pointed needles (or one size smaller than size needed to achieve gauge)

Optional Magic Loop: circular needle in sizes above, at least 40" (101 cm) long for HAT or 32" (81 cm) long for MITTENS

Circular stitch markers

Small stitch holder (or waste yarn)

Yarn needle for weaving in ends

## BERRY STITCH HAT: Finished Size and Dimensions

| Finished Size | Hat Circumference | Finished Hat Height |
|---|---|---|
| Average Male Head: 22" (56 cm) to 24" (61 cm) | 22" (56 cm) | 9" (23 cm) |

## BERRY STITCH HAT

### CAST ON STITCHES
### AND BEGIN KNITTING

*Note that stitch count does not stay consistent while working the berry stitch pattern at the beginning.*

Using smaller circular needle and yarn A doubled, cast on 120 stitches. Place BOR marker and join in the round being careful not to twist (see page 20).

**Round 1:** *K3, p1*; repeat from * to * to end of round.

**Rounds 2–7:** Repeat round 1 six times. Do not cut yarn A.

**Round 8:** Change to larger needles and yarn B, knit.

**Round 9:** With yarn B, knit.

**Round 10:** With yarn A, *sl3 wyib, [k, yo, k] into next stitch*; repeat from * to * to end of round.

**Round 11:** With yarn A, *sl3 wyib, p3*; repeat from * to * to end of round.

**Round 12:** With yarn B, *sl1, k2tog, psso, sl3 wyib*; repeat from * to * to end of round.

**Round 13:** With yarn B, *[k, yo, k] into next stitch, sl3 wyib*; repeat from * to * to end of round.

**Round 14:** With yarn A, *sl3 wyib, p3*; repeat from * to * to end of round.

**Round 15:** With yarn A, *sl3 wyib, p3tog*; repeat from * to * to end of round.

**Round 16:** With yarn B, *K3, p1*; repeat from * to * to end of round.

**Rounds 17–18:** Repeat round 16 twice.

**Rounds 19–29:** Repeat rounds 8–18.

**Rounds 30–37:** Repeat rounds 8–15.

(continued)

Cut yarn A leaving a tail at least 8"
(20 cm) long to weave in later. From this
point on only yarn B is used.

**Round 38:** With yarn B, *k3, p1*; repeat
from * to * to end of round.

Repeat round 38 until length from
cast-on row measures approximately
6¾" (17 cm).

### SHAPE TOP

Work decreases to shape the crown of
the hat. Change to DPNs when stitches
will no longer fit comfortably around the
circular needle.

**Round 1:** *Ssk, k1, p1*; repeat from * to *
to end of round—90 sts remain.

**Round 2:** *K2, p1*; repeat from * to *
to end of round.

**Rounds 3–4:** Repeat round 2 twice.

**Round 5:** *K2tog, p1*; repeat from * to *
to end of round—60 sts remain.

**Round 6:** *K1, p1*; repeat from * to *
to end of round.

**Rounds 7–8:** Repeat round 6 twice.

**Round 9:** *K2tog*; repeat from * to *
to end of round—30 sts remain.

**Round 10:** Knit.

**Rounds 11–12:** Repeat round 10 twice.

**Round 13:** *K2tog*; repeat from * to *
to end of round—15 sts remain.

**Round 14:** Knit.

**Round 15:** *K2tog*; repeat from * to *
until 8 sts remain.

To finish the hat, cut the yarn leaving
a tail at least 8" (20 cm) long. Using a
yarn needle thread the tail through the
remaining stitches and pass through the
hole in the top of the hat to the inside.
Pull the tail firmly to close the hole and
weave the ends into the stitches on the
inside of the hat to secure. Weave in all
ends and steam lightly.

| BERRY STITCH MITTENS: Finished Size and Dimensions | | |
| --- | --- | --- |
| **Finished Size** | **Hand Circumference** | **Finished Mitten Length** |
| Average Male Hand: 8½" (22 cm) to 9½" (24 cm) | 8" (20 cm) | 11" (28 cm) |

# BERRY STITCH MITTENS

*The berry stitch pattern is quite elastic
and will fit a wide range of hands but if
you want to change the fit a bit more, use a
needle either one size smaller or bigger. The
length can be adjusted in the ribbing section
after the gusset is completed.*

### CAST ON STITCHES AND MAKE RIBBED CUFF

*Note that stitch count does not stay
consistent while working the berry
stitch pattern.*

Right and left mittens are worked
the same.

Using smaller needles and yarn A
doubled, cast on 48 stitches. Place BOR
marker and join in the round being
careful not to twist (see page 20).

**Round 1:** *K3, p1*; repeat from * to *
to end of round.

Repeat round 1 until cuff measures
2¼" (5.5 cm). Do not cut yarn A.

### MAIN PORTION OF MITTEN

**Round 1:** Change to larger needles and
yarn B, knit.

**Round 2:** With yarn B, knit.

**Round 3:** With yarn A, *sl3 wyib, [k, yo, k] into next stitch*; repeat from * to * to end of round.

**Round 4:** With yarn A, *sl3 wyib, p3*; repeat from * to * to end of round.

**Round 5:** With yarn B, *sl1, k2tog, psso, sl3 wyib*; repeat from * to * to end of round.

**Round 6:** With yarn B, *[k, yo, k] into next stitch, sl3 wyib*; repeat from * to * to end of round.

**Round 7:** With yarn A, *sl3 wyib, p3*; repeat from * to * to end of round.

**Round 8:** With yarn A, *sl3 wyib, p3tog*; repeat from * to * to end of round.

   Cut yarn A leaving a tail at least 8" (20 cm) long. From this point on only yarn B is used.

**Round 9:** With yarn B, *k3, p1*; repeat from * to * to end of round.

**Round 10:** Repeat round 9.

## MAKE THUMB GUSSET

**Round 11:** [K3, p1] 5 times, k4, pm, inc 1, pm, [k3, p1] to end of round.

**Round 12:** [K3, p1] 5 times, k4, sm, k1, sm, [k3, p1] to end of round.

**Round 13:** [K3, p1] 5 times, k4, sm, M1L, k1, M1R, sm, [k3, p1] to end of round—3 sts between gusset markers.

**Round 14:** [K3, p1] 5 times, k4, sm, knit to next marker, sm, [k3,p1] to end of round.

**Round 15:** [K3, p1] 5 times, k4, sm, M1L, knit to next marker, M1R, sm, [k3,p1] to end of round—5 sts between gusset markers.

**Round 16:** Repeat round 14.

**Round 17:** [K3, p1] 5 times, k4, sm, M1L, knit to next marker, M1R, sm, [k3,p1] to end of round—7 sts between gusset markers.

**Round 18–19:** Repeat round 14 twice.

**Round 20:** [K3, p1] 5 times, k4, sm, M1L, knit to next marker, M1R, sm,

[k3,p1] to end of round—9 sts between gusset markers.

**Rounds 21–22:** Repeat round 14 twice.

**Round 23:** [K3, p1] 5 times, k4, sm, M1L, knit to next marker, M1R, sm, [k3,p1] to end of round—11 sts between gusset markers.

**Rounds 24–25:** Repeat round 14 twice.

**Round 26:** [K3, p1] 5 times, k4, sm, M1L, knit to next marker, M1R, sm, [k3,p1] to end of round—13 sts between gusset markers.

**Rounds 27–28:** Repeat round 14 twice.

**Round 29:** [K3, p1] 5 times, k4, sm, M1L, knit to next marker, M1R, sm, [k3,p1] to end of round—15 sts between gusset markers.

**Rounds 30–32:** Repeat round 14 three times.

**Round 33:** [K3, p1] 5 times, k4, sm, M1L, knit to next marker, M1R, sm, [k3,p1] to end of round—17 sts between gusset markers.

(continued)

**Round 34:** Repeat round 14.

**Round 35:** [K3, p1] six times, remove marker, transfer next 17 sts (thumb gusset) to st holder, remove marker, cast on one stitch using backwards thumb loop to cover gap left by thumb gusset, [k3, p1] to end of round.

**Round 36:** [K3, p1] six times, p1, [k3, p1] to end of round.

**Rounds 37–41:** Repeat round 30.

**Round 42:** [K3, p1] five times, k3, p2tog, [k3, p1] to end of round.

**Round 43:** *K3, p1*; repeat from * to * to end of round.

Repeat round 43 until total length from cast-on row equals 9" (23 cm).

### SHAPE TIP OF MITTEN

Work decreases to shape the tip of the mittens.

**Round 1:** *K1, ssk, p1, [k3, p1] four times, k1, k2tog, k1*; repeat from * to * once—44 sts remain.

**Round 2:** *K2, p1, [k3, p1] four times, k3*; repeat from * to * one time.

**Round 3:** *K1, ssk, [k3, p1] four times, k2tog, k1*; repeat from * to * once—40 sts remain.

**Round 4:** *K2, [k3, p1] four times, k2*; repeat from * to * one time.

**Round 5:** *K1, ssk, k2, p1, [k3, p1] two times, k3, k2tog, k1*; repeat from * to * once—36 sts remain.

**Round 6:** *K4, p1, [k3, p1] two times, k5*; repeat from * to * one time.

**Round 7:** * K1, ssk, k1, p1, [k3, p1] two times, k2, k2tog, k1*; repeat from * to * once—32 sts remain.

**Round 8:** *[K3, p1] three times, k4*; repeat from * to * one time.

**Round 9:** *K1, ssk, p1, [k3, p1] two times, k1, k2tog, k1*; repeat from * to * once—28 sts remain.

**Round 10:** *K1, ssk, [k3, p1] two times, k2tog, k1*; repeat from * to * once—24 sts remain.

**Round 11:** *K1, ssk, k2, p1, k3, k2tog, k1*; repeat from * to * once—20 sts remain.

**Round 12:** *K1, ssk, k1, p1, k2, k2tog, k1*; repeat from * to * once—16 sts remain.

**Round 13:** *K1, ssk, p1, k1, k2tog, k1*; repeat from * to * once—12 sts remain.

### FINISHING MAIN PORTION OF MITTEN

Cut yarn leaving a tail at least 8" (20 cm) long. Thread tail onto yarn needle and draw through remaining stitches on needle. Pull to tighten loop and pass yarn needle to inside of mitten and weave yarn tail through stitches to secure.

### MITTEN THUMB

Remove gusset stitches from stitch holder and distribute on three larger DPNs. Attach yarn leaving a tail at least 8' (20 cm) long, pick up and knit 2 stitches over gap. Place marker to indicate beginning of round, join in the round and continue to knit as follows:

**Round 1:** K17, k2tog—18 sts.

**Round 2:** Knit.

**Rounds 3–10:** Repeat round 2. Length from beginning of thumb should equal about 1¾" (4.5 cm).

**Round 11:** *K2tog, k4*; repeat from * to * to end of round—15 sts remain.

**Round 12:** Knit.

**Round 13:** *K2tog, k3*; repeat from * to * to end of round—12 sts remain.

**Round 14:** Knit.

**Round 15:** *K2tog, k2*; repeat from * to * to end of round—9 sts remain.

**Round 16:** *K2tog, k1*; repeat from * to * to end of round—6 sts remain.

### FINISH THUMB

Cut yarn leaving a tail at least 8" (20 cm) long. Thread tail onto yarn needle and draw through remaining stitches on needle. Pull to tighten loop and pass to inside of thumb and weave through stitches to secure. Using yarn tail at the base of the thumb, close any gaps that might remain and secure by weaving through stitches. To finish mittens weave in all other ends and steam lightly.

# String of Purls Hat and Fingerless Mittens for Women

This is an adaptation of the berry stitch pattern used in the men's hat and mittens. I think the berries look like a string of pearls (purls) against a sky blue background.

Knitting with the background yarn was a real treat. It's hand-dyed baby alpaca and it's beautifully soft and supple. I also love the semi-solid color. It makes the hat and mittens even prettier and it makes a beautiful foundation for the pearls. The pearls are made from a lovely undyed alpaca and wool blend yarn. The hat and mittens are sized to fit an average adult female but notes for adjusting the sizes are included.

## GAUGE

26 sts and 28 rows = 4" (10 cm) in k3, p1 ribbing

*The gauge is the same for both the hat and the mittens.*

## YARN

Yarn A: Light weight smooth yarn, HAT: 130 yd (119 m), MITTENS: 130 yd (119 m)

Shown: Shibui Knits Baby Alpaca DK, 100% baby alpaca; 250 yd (230 m) per 3.5 oz (100 g) skein, color #5483 Rapids, 1 skein

Yarn B: Light weight smooth yarn, HAT: 30 yd (27 m), MITTENS: 30 yd (27 m)

Shown: Berroco *Ultra Alpaca Light*, 50% alpaca, 50% wool; 144 yd (132 m) per 1.75 oz (50 g) ball, color #4201 Winter White, 1 skein

*1 skein each is sufficient for both the hat and the mittens.*

## NEEDLES AND NOTIONS

US size 6 (4 mm) 16" (41 cm) circular needle or size needed to achieve gauge

US size 4 (3.5 mm) 16" (41 cm) circular needle (or two sizes smaller than size needed to achieve gauge)

US size 6 (4 mm) double-pointed needles or size needed to achieve gauge

Optional Magic Loop: circular needle in above needle sizes, at least 40" (101 cm) long for HAT or 32" (81 cm) long for MITTENS

Circular stitch markers

Small stitch holder (or waste yarn)

Yarn needle for weaving in ends

| STRING OF PURLS HAT: Finished Size and Dimensions | | |
| --- | --- | --- |
| **Finished Size** | **Hat Circumference** | **Finished Hat Height** |
| Average Female Head: 19" (48.5 cm) to 21" (53.5 cm) | 18½" (47 cm) | 8" (20 cm) |

## STRING OF PURLS HAT

The stitch pattern for the hat is a multiple of four stitches. If you would like to make the hat larger or smaller then add or subtract to the number of cast-on stitches in a multiple of four. For instance for a smaller hat, cast on 112 stitches or for a larger hat cast on 124 or 128 stitches. You will also need to change the length appropriately.

### CAST ON STITCHES AND BEGIN KNITTING

*Note that stitch count does not stay consistent while working the berry stitch pattern at the beginning.*

Using smaller circular needle and yarn A, cast on 120 stitches. Place BOR marker and join in the round being careful not to twist (see page 20).

(continued)

**Round 1:** *K3, p1*; repeat from * to * to end of round.

**Rounds 2–9:** Repeat round 1 eight times. Change to larger needles.

**Round 10:** Knit.

**Round 11:** Repeat round 10.

**Round 12:** With yarn B, *sl3 wyib, [k, yo, k] into next stitch*; repeat from * to * to end of round.

**Round 13:** With yarn B, *sl3 wyib, p3*; repeat from * to * to end of round.

**Round 14:** With yarn A, *sl1, k2tog, psso, sl3 wyib*; repeat from * to * to end of round.

**Round 15:** With yarn A, *[k, yo, k] into next stitch, sl3 wyib*; repeat from * to * to end of round.

**Round 16:** With yarn B, *sl3 wyib, p3*; repeat from * to * to end of round.

**Round 17:** With yarn B, *sl3 wyib, p3tog*; repeat from * to * to end of round.

**Round 18:** With yarn A, *k3, p1*; repeat from * to * to end of round.

**Round 19:** With yarn A, knit.

**Round 20:** Repeat round 19.

**Rounds 21–26:** Repeat rounds 12–17.

Cut yarn B leaving a tail at least 8" (20 cm) long to weave in later.

**Round 27:** With yarn A, *k3, p1*; repeat from * to * to end of round.

Repeat round 27 until length from cast-on row is 5½" (14 cm).

## SHAPE TOP

Finish decorative section and work decreases to shape the crown of the hat.

**Round 1:** With yarn B, *sl3 wyib, [k, yo, k] into next stitch*; repeat from * to * to end of round.

**Round 2:** With yarn B, *sl3 wyib, p3*; repeat from * to * to end of round.

**Round 3:** With yarn A, *s1, k2tog, psso, sl3 wyib*; repeat from * to * to end of round.

**Round 4:** With yarn A, *[k, yo, k] into next stitch, sl3 wyib*; repeat from * to * to end of round.

**Round 5:** With yarn B, *sl3 wyib, p3*; repeat from * to * to end of round.

**Round 6:** With yarn B, *sl3 wyib, p3tog*; repeat from * to * to end of round.

Discontinue yarn B and finish hat with yarn A only.

**Round 7:** With yarn A, *k3, p1*; repeat from * to * to end of round.

**Round 8:** Repeat round 7.

**Round 9:** *Ssk, k1, p1*; repeat from * to * to end of round—90 sts remain.

**Round 10:** *K2, p1*; repeat from * to * to end of round.

**Round 11–12:** Repeat round 10 twice.

**Round 13:** *K2tog, p1*; repeat from * to * to end of round—60 sts remain.

**Round 14:** *K1, p1*; repeat from * to * to end of round.

**Round 15:** Repeat round 14.

**Round 16:** *Ssk*; repeat from * to * to end of round—30 sts remain.

**Round 17:** Knit.

**Round 18:** *K2tog*; repeat from * to * to end of round—15 sts remain.

To finish the hat, cut the yarn leaving a tail at least 8" (20 cm) long. Using a yarn needle, thread the tail through the remaining stitches and pass through the hole in the top of the hat to the inside. Pull the tail firmly to close the hole and weave the ends into the stitches on the inside of the hat to secure. Weave in all ends.

## STRING OF PURLS MITTENS: Finished Size and Dimensions

| Finished Size | Hand Circumference | Finished Mitten Length |
|---|---|---|
| Average Female Hand: 6½" (16.5 cm) to 7½" (19 cm) | 6" (15 cm) | 7" (18 cm) |

# STRING OF PURLS MITTENS

The stitch for the mittens is quite elastic and will fit a wide range of hands but if you would like to change the fit a bit more then use a needle either one size smaller or bigger. The length can be adjusted in the section following the third string of pearls after the gusset is completed.

### CAST ON STITCHES AND MAKE CUFF

Right and left mittens are worked the same.

*Note that stitch count does not stay consistent while working the berry stitch pattern at the beginning.*

Using smaller circular needle and yarn A, cast on 40 stitches. Place BOR marker and join in the round being careful not to twist (see page 20).

**Round 1:** *K3, p1*; repeat from * to * to end of round.

**Rounds 2–9:** Repeat round 1 eight times.

Change to large needle.

**Round 10:** Knit.

**Round 11:** Repeat round 10.

**Round 12:** With yarn B, *sl3 wyib, [k, yo, k] into next stitch*; repeat from * to * to end of round.

**Round 13:** With yarn B, *sl3 wyib, p3*; repeat from * to * to end of round.

**Round 14:** With yarn A, *sl1, k2tog, psso, sl3 wyib*; repeat from * to * to end of round.

(continued)

**Round 15:** With yarn A, *[k, yo, k] into next stitch, sl3 wyib*; repeat from * to * to end of round.

**Round 16:** With yarn B, *sl3 wyib, p3*; repeat from * to * to end of round.

**Round 17:** With yarn B, *sl3 wyib, p3tog*; repeat from * to * to end of round.

**Round 18:** With yarn A, *k3, p1*; repeat from * to * to end of round.

**Round 19:** With yarn A, knit.

**Round 20:** Repeat round 19.

**Rounds 21–26:** Repeat rounds 12–17.

Cut yarn B leaving a tail at least 8" (20 cm) long to weave in later.

**Round 27:** With yarn A, *k3, p1*; repeat from * to * to end of round.

### MAKE THUMB GUSSET

**Round 28:** [K3, p1] four times, k4, pm, M1L, pm, *k3, p1; repeat from * to * to end of round.

**Round 29:** [K3, p1] four times, k4, sm, M1L, k1, M1R, sm, *k3, p1*; repeat from * to * to end of round—3 sts between markers.

**Round 30:** [K3, p1] four times, k4, sm, knit to next marker, sm, *k3, p1*; repeat from * to * to end of round.

**Round 31:** [K3, p1] four times, k4, sm, M1L, k to next marker, M1R, sm, *k3, p1*; repeat from * to * to end of round—5 sts between markers.

**Round 32–33:** Repeat round 30 twice.

**Round 34:** [K3, p1] four times, k4, sm, M1L, k to next marker, M1R, sm, *k3, p1*; repeat from * to * to end of round—7 sts between markers.

**Rounds 35–36:** Repeat round 30 twice.

**Round 37:** [K3, p1] four times, k4, sm, M1L, k to next marker, M1R, sm, *k3, p1*; repeat from * to * to end of round—9 sts between markers.

**Rounds 38–39:** Repeat round 30.

**Round 40:** [K3, p1] four times, k4, sm, M1L, k to next marker, M1R, sm, *k3, p1*; repeat from * to * to end of round—11 sts between markers.

**Rounds 41–42:** Repeat round 30.

**Round 43:** [K3, p1] four times, k4, sm, M1L, k to next marker, M1R, sm, *k3, p1*; repeat from * to * to end of round—13 sts between markers.

**Round 44:** [K3, p1] four times, k4, remove marker, place next 13 sts on holder, remove marker, use backwards thumb loop to cast on 1 st over gap left by gusset stitches, *k3, p1*; repeat from * to * to end of round.

**Round 45:** Knit.

**Round 46:** K19, k2tog, k20—40 sts remain.

Rejoin yarn B and continue as follows:

**Round 47:** With yarn B, *sl3 wyib, [k, yo, k] into next stitch*; repeat from * to * to end of round.

**Round 48:** With yarn B, *sl3 wyib, p3*; repeat from * to * to end of round.

**Round 49:** With yarn A, *sl1, k2tog, psso, sl3 wyib*; repeat from * to * to end of round.

**Round 50:** With yarn A, *[k, yo, k] into next stitch, sl3 wyib*; repeat from * to * to end of round.

**Round 51:** With yarn B, *sl3 wyib, p3*; repeat from * to * to end of round.

**Round 52:** With yarn B, *sl3 wyib, p3tog*; repeat from * to * to end of round.

**Round 53:** With yarn A, *k3, p1*; repeat from * to * to end of round.

**Round 54:** Repeat round 53.

Bind off in pattern using the k3, p1 sequence.

### MITTEN THUMB

Remove gusset stitches from stitch holder and distribute on three larger double-pointed needles. Attach yarn leaving an 8" (20 cm) tail, pick up and knit 3 stitches over gap. Place marker to indicate beginning of round, join in the round and continue to knit as follows:

**Round 1:** K12, k2tog, k2—15 sts remain.

**Rounds 2–5:** Knit to end of round.

Bind off loosely.

To finish mittens weave in all other ends and steam lightly.

# Elegant Cables Hat and Fingerless Mittens for Women

This is one of those yarns that makes me wish I could include a sample in every book. It is so soft and silky that you really need to feel it to believe it. The unique chained structure of the yarn creates items that are very light and airy and is also ideal for texture stitches such as the simple cables used in this pattern. If you want to substitute a different yarn, choose one with mostly alpaca which tends to be softer and lighter in weight than wool.

The fit of the hat is snug and flattering and the mittens have a long cuff that can either be turned down for a cute look or left long and worn up your coat sleeve to keep you toasty warm when the wind blows. The pattern is written to fit an average size woman but notes are included to modify the fit to smaller or bigger sizes. The cable pattern and this unique yarn are both very elastic, so even though the hat looks skinny when lying flat it actually expands easily.

## GAUGE

22 sts = 4" (10 cm) in stockinette stitch

25 sts = 4" (10 cm) in cable pattern

*The gauge is the same for both the hat and the mittens.*

## YARN

Yarn A: Medium weight smooth yarn, HAT: 25 yd (23 m), MITTENS: 55 yd (50 m)

Shown: Rowan *Lima*, 84% baby alpaca, 8% merino wool, 8% nylon; 109 yd (100 m) per 1.75 oz (50 g) skein, Nazca, #887, HAT: 1 skein, MITTENS: 1 skein

Yarn B: Medium weight smooth yarn, HAT: 109 yd (100 m), MITTENS: 65 yd (59 m)

Shown: Rowan *Lima*, Machu Picchu, #885, HAT: 1 skein, MITTENS: 1 skein

*To make both the hat and the mittens, you will need 1 skein of yarn A and 2 skeins of yarn B.*

## NEEDLES AND NOTIONS

HAT: US size 8 (5 mm) 16" (40 cm) circular needle or size needed to achieve gauge

US size 8 (5 mm) double-pointed needles or size needed to achieve gauge

MITTENS: US size 8 (5 mm) double-pointed needles or size needed to achieve gauge

US size 7 (4.55 mm) double-pointed needles (or one size smaller than size needed to achieve gauge)

Optional Magic Loop: circular needle in above needle sizes, at least 40" (101 cm) long for HAT or 32" (81 cm) long for MITTENS

Circular stitch markers

Cable needle

Small stitch holder (or waste yarn)

Yarn needle for weaving in ends

## ABBREVIATIONS

4-st RKC = Slip next 2 sts purlwise to cable needle and hold at back of work, knit next 2 sts from left needle then knit 2 sts from cable needle.

6-st RKC: = Slip next 3 sts purlwise to cable needle and hold at back of work, knit next 3 sts from left needle then knit 3 sts from cable needle.

M1RP = Make 1 right purlwise

M1LP = Make 1 left purlwise

For all other abbreviations see page 144.

## ELEGANT CABLES HAT: Finished Size and Dimensions

| Finished Size | Hat Circumference | Finished Hat Height |
|---|---|---|
| Average Female Head: 19" (48.5 cm) to 21" (53.5 cm) | 14" (35.6 cm) | 9" (23 cm) |

# ELEGANT CABLES HAT

The cable pattern for the hat is a multiple of 11 stitches. If you would like to make the hat larger or smaller, add or subtract to the number of cast-on stitches in a multiple of 11. For instance for a smaller hat, cast on 77 stitches or for a larger hat cast on 99 stitches. You will also need to change the length appropriately.

## CAST ON STITCHES AND BEGIN KNITTING

Using circular needle and yarn A, cast on 88 stitches. Place BOR marker and join in the round being careful not to twist (see page 20). Change to DPNs when the stitches will no longer fit comfortably around the circular needle.

(continued)

**Round 1:** *K2, p2, k2, p1, k1, p1, k1, p1*; repeat from * to * to end of round.

**Rounds 2–4:** Repeat round 1. Cut yarn A leaving a tail at least 8" (20 cm) long to weave in later.

Change to yarn B and continue as follows:

**Round 5:** *K6, p1, k1, p1, k1, p1*; repeat from * to * to end of round.

**Rounds 6–7:** repeat round 5 twice.

**Round 8:** *6-st RKC, p1, k1, p1, k1, p1*; repeat from * to * to end of round.

**Rounds 9–15:** Repeat round 5 seven times.

**Rounds 16–39:** Repeat rounds 8–15 three times.

**Round 40:** Repeat round 8.

**Rounds 41–46:** Repeat round 5 six times.

**Round 47:** *K6, p1, k1, k2tog, p1*; repeat from * to * to end of round— 80 sts remain.

**Round 48:** *6-st RKC, p1, k2, p1*; repeat from * to * to end of round.

**Round 49:** *K6, p1, k2, p1*; repeat from * to * to end of round.

**Round 50:** *K4, k2tog, p1, k2, p1*; repeat from * to * to end of round— 72 sts remain.

**Round 51:** *K5, p1, k2, p1*; repeat from * to * to end of round.

**Round 52:** *Ssk, k3, p1, k2, p1*; repeat from * to * to end of round— 64 sts remain.

**Round 53:** * K4, p1, k2, p1*; repeat from * to * to end of round.

**Round 54:** Repeat round 53.

**Round 55:** *K4, p1, k2tog, p1*; repeat from * to * to end of round— 56 sts remain.

**Round 56:** *2-st RKC, p1, k1, p1*; repeat from * to * to end of round.

**Round 57:** *K2, k2tog, k1, p1, k1*; repeat from * to * to end of round— 48 sts remain.

**Round 58:** *K3, p1, k1, p1*; repeat from * to * to end of round.

**Round 59:** *Ssk, k1, p1, k1, p1*; repeat from * to * to end of round— 40 sts remain.

**Round 60:** *K2, p1, k1, p1*; repeat from * to * to end of round.

**Round 61:** *K2tog, p1, k1, p1*; repeat from * to * to end of round— 32 sts remain.

**Round 62:** *K1, p1*; repeat from * to * to end of round.

**Round 63:** *Ssk, k1, p1*; repeat from * to * to end of round—24 sts remain.

**Round 64:** *K2tog, p1*; repeat from * to * to end of round—16 sts remain.

**Round 65:** *K2tog*; repeat from * to * to end of round—8 sts remain.

To finish the hat, cut the yarn leaving a tail at least 8" (20 cm) long. Using a yarn needle, thread the tail through the remaining stitches and pass through the hole in the top of the hat to the inside. Pull the tail firmly to close the hole and weave the ends into the stitches on the inside of the hat to secure. Weave in all ends.

## ELEGANT CABLES MITTENS: Finished Size and Dimensions

| Finished Size | Hand Circumference | Finished Mitten Length |
| --- | --- | --- |
| Average Female Hand: 6½" (16.5 cm) to 7½" (19 cm) | 5" (13 cm) | 8¾" (22 cm) |

# ELEGANT CABLES MITTENS

The cable pattern is quite elastic, but if you would like to change the fit a bit more, then use a needle either one size smaller or bigger. The length can be adjusted in the long ribbing section or by making the final dark band shorter or longer.

### CAST ON STITCHES
### AND MAKE RIBBED CUFF

Right and left mittens are worked the same.

Using smaller needles and yarn A, cast on 36 sts. Place BOR marker and join in the round being careful not to twist (see page 20).

**Round 1:** *K2, p2, k2, p1, k1, p1*; repeat from * to * to end of round.

Continue round 1 until length from cast-on edge is approximately 4" (10 cm). Cut yarn A leaving a tail at least 8" (20 cm) long to weave in later.

### MAKE GUSSET FOR THUMB

Change to larger needles and yarn B.

**Round 1:** *K6, p1, k1, p1*; repeat from * to * to end of round.

**Round 2:** Repeat round 1.

(continued)

**Round 3:** K6, p1, k1, p1, k6, p1, pm, M1R, k1, M1L, pm, p1, [k6, p1, k1, p1] twice—3 sts between markers.

**Round 4:** K6, p1, k1, p1, k6, p1, sm, k3, sm, p1, [k6, p1, k1, p1] twice.

**Round 5:** 6-st RKC, p1, k1, p1, 6-st RKC, p1, sm, k1, M1RP, k1, M1LP, k1, sm, p1, [6-st RKC, p1, k1, p1] twice— 5 sts between markers.

**Round 6:** K6, p1, k1, p1, k6, p1, sm, k1, p1, k1, p1, k1, sm, p1, [k6, p1, k1, p1] twice.

**Round 7:** K6, p1, k1, p1, k6, p1, sm, k1, p1, M1R, k1, M1L, p1, k1, sm, p1, [k6, p1, k1, p1] twice—7 sts between markers.

**Round 8:** K6, p1, k1, p1, k6, p, sm, k1, p1, k3, p1, k1, sm, p1, [k6, p1, k1, p1] twice.

**Round 9:** Repeat round 8.

**Round 10:** K6, p1, k1, p1, k6, p1, sm k1, p1, k1, M1RP, k1, M1LP, k1, p1, k1, sm, p1, [k6, p1, k1, p1] twice— 9 sts between markers.

**Round 11:** K6, p1, k1, p1, k6, p1, sm, [k1, p1] four times, k1, sm, p1, [k6, p1, k1, p1] twice.

**Round 12:** Repeat round 11.

**Round 13:** 6-st RKC, p1, k1, p1, 6-st RKC, p1, sm, [k1, p1] twice, M1R, k1, M1L, [p1, k1] twice, sm, p1, [6-st RKC, p1, k1, p1] twice— 11 sts between markers.

**Round 14:** K6, p1, k1, p1, k6, p1, sm, [k1, p1] twice, k3, [p1, k1] twice, sm, p1, [k6, p1, k1, p1] twice.

**Round 15:** Repeat round 14.

**Round 16:** K6, p1, k1, p1, k6, p1, sm, [k1, p1] twice, k1, M1RP, k1, M1LP, k1, [p1, k1] twice, sm, p1, [k6, p1, k1, p1] twice—13 sts between markers.

**Round 17:** K6, p1, k1, p1, k6, p1, sm, [k1, p1] six times, k1, sm, p1, [k6, p1, k1, p1] twice.

**Round 18:** Repeat round 17.

**Round 19:** K6, p1, k1, p1, k6, p1, sm, [k1, p1] three times, M1R, k1, M1L, [p1, k1] three times, sm, p1, [k6, p1, k1, p1] twice— 15 sts between markers.

**Round 20:** K6, p1, k1, p1, k6, p1, sm, [k1, p1] three times, k3, [p1, k1] three times, sm, p1, [k6, p1, k1, p1] twice.

**Round 21:** 6-st RKC, p1, k1, p1, 6-st RKC, p1, sm, [k1, p1] three times, k3, [p1, k1] three times, sm, p1, [6-st RKC, p1, k1, p1] twice.

**Round 22:** K6, p1, k1, p1, k6, p1, remove marker, place next 15 sts on holder, remove marker, use backwards thumb loop to cast on 1 st over gap left by gusset stitches, p1, [k6, p1, k1, p1] twice— 36 sts remain.

**Round 23:** *K6, p1, k1, p1*; repeat from * to * to end of round.

**Rounds 24–28:** Repeat round 23 five times.

**Round 29:** *6-st RKC, p1, k1, p1*; repeat from * to * to end of round.

**Round 30:** Repeat round 23.
Cut yarn B leaving a tail at least 8" (20 cm) long to weave in later.
    Change to yarn A.

**Round 31:** *K2, p2, k2, p1, k1, p1*; repeat from * to * to end of round.

**Rounds 32–34:** Repeat row 31 three times.
    Bind off loosely in pattern using k2, p2, k2, p1, k1, p1 sequence.

### MITTEN THUMB

Remove gusset stitches from stitch holder and distribute on three larger DPNs. Attach yarn B leaving a tail at least 8" (20 cm) long, pick up and knit 2 stitches over gap (if you would prefer a contrast edge on the thumb, then use yarn A for this section instead). Place BOR marker, join in the round and continue to knit as follows:

**Round 1:** [K1, p1] three times, k3, [p1, k1] three times, p2tog—16 sts remain.

**Round 2:** [K1, p1] three times, k3, [p1, k1] three times, p1.

**Rounds 3–5:** Repeat round 2 three times.
    Bind off loosely in pattern. Using yarn tail at the base of the thumb, close any gaps that might remain and secure by weaving through stitches. Weave in all other ends to finish.

# Hat Nation

You can make this hat for just about anybody and the pattern stays the same, 80 easy stitches in rib with a neat decrease at the crown. The size is varied by changing the weight of yarn. Chunky yarn works well for adults, heavy worsted makes a perfect kid's hat, and light worsted will give you the cutest baby hat.

You can expand the choices even further by making the height either short or tall. The short version will fit like a skull cap ('skully' to the younger set). Make it taller and you can wear it as a slouch cap, movie star style, or a watch cap which is perfect for ice fishing in Minnesota.

That's why I call it hat nation—one pattern can fit just about anyone! Help build the population, and try different yarns to make your own versions.

Because this stitch pattern is very flexible, gauge isn't as important compared to other designs. Generally speaking you should use a needle size that is two sizes smaller than specified on the ball band. However, if you want to experiment further or obtain a size that is different than shown below then by all means, try a smaller or larger needle.

### GAUGE

Size 1: 35 sts = 4" (10 cm) in k2, p2 ribbing

Size 2: 29 sts = 4" (10 cm) in k2, p2 ribbing

Size 3: 21 sts = 4" (10 cm) in k2, p2 ribbing

### YARN

The yarn weight and approximate yardage for each hat is shown in the chart above.

Shown:

Size 1: Plymouth Yarn *Baby Boutique*, 50% microfiber, 50% nylon; 104 yd (95) m per 1.75 oz (50 g) ball, color #04, 1 ball

Size 2: Nashua Yarns *Snowbird*, 70% wool, 30% alpaca; 73 yd (67 m) per 1.75 oz (50 g) ball, color #2201 Aqua, 2 balls

Size 3S: Classic Elite Yarns *Ariosa*, 90% merino wool, 10% cashmere; 87 yd (80 m) per 1.75 oz (50 g) ball, color 4814 Slate Gray, 2 balls

Size 3T: Classic Elite Yarns *Ariosa*, 90% merino wool, 10% cashmere; 87 yd (80 m) per 1.75 oz (50 g) ball, color 4809 Aquarius, 2 balls

### NEEDLES AND NOTIONS

16" (40 cm) circular and double-pointed needles in the sizes shown below:

Size 1: US size 5 (3.75 mm)

Size 2: US size 7 (4.5 mm)

Size 3: US size 9 (5.5 mm)

Optional Magic Loop: above needle sizes in a circular needle at least 40" (101 cm) long.

Circular stitch marker

Yarn needle for weaving in ends

Size 3T: Blue adult hat
(hat shown is tall height)

Size 3S: Grey adult hat
(hat shown is short height)

Size 1: Yellow baby hat
(hat shown is tall height)

Size 2: Aqua tweed kid's hat
(hat shown is tall height)

## HAT NATION HAT: Size, Finished Dimensions, and Yardage

|  | Yarn Weight | Finished Hat Circumference | To Fit Head Circumference | Finished Hat Height | Approximate Yardage |
|---|---|---|---|---|---|
| Size 1 | Medium (Ligt Worsted) | 9" (23 cm) | 12" (30 cm) to 15" (38 cm) | 7" (18 cm) to 8½" (22 cm) | 100 yd (91 m) to 125 yd (114 m) |
| Size 2 | Medium (Heavy Worsted) | 11" (28 cm) | 17" (43 cm) to 20" (51 cm) | 8½" (22 cm) to 11" (28 cm) | 95 yd (87 m) to 130 yd (119 m) |
| Size 3T | Bulky (Chunky) - Tall Version | 15" (38 cm) | 20" (51 cm) to 22½" (57 cm) | 9" (23 cm) to 12" (30 cm) | 140 yd (128 m) to 185 yd (269 m) |

# HAT NATION HAT

### CAST ON STITCHES AND BEGIN KNITTING

Using circular needle, cast on 80 stitches. Place BOR marker and join in the round being careful not to twist (see page 20).

**Round 1:** *K2, p2*; repeat from * to * to end of round.

Repeat round 1 until length from cast-on row equals desired height as shown in chart below:

|  | Short Hat Height Before Shaping | Tall Hat Height Before Shaping |
|---|---|---|
| Size 1 | 5" (13 cm) | 6" (15 cm) to 6½" (17 cm) |
| Size 2 | 6" (15 cm) | 7" (18 cm) to 8" (20 cm) |
| Size 3 | 7" (18 cm) | 8" (20 cm) to 10" (25 cm) |

### SHAPE TOP

Change to DPNs when the stitches no longer fit comfortably around the circular needle.

**Round 1:** *[K2, p2] twice, k2tog, p2, [k2, p2] twice*; repeat from * to * to end of round—76 sts remain.

**Round 2:** *K2, p2, k2, p2tog, k1, p2tog, [k2, p2] twice*; repeat from * to * to end of round—68 sts remain.

**Round 3:** *K2, p2, k2, [k2tog] twice, k1, p2, k2, p2*; repeat from * to * to end of round—60 sts remain.

**Round 4:** *K2, p2, ssk, k1, k2tog, p2, k2, p2, *; repeat from * to * to end of round—52 sts remain.

**Round 5:** *K2, p2, k3tog, p2, k2, p2*; repeat from * to * to end of round—44 sts remain.

**Round 6:** *K2, p2tog, k1, p2tog, k2, p2*; repeat from * to * to end of round—36 sts remain.

**Round 7:** *K2, [k2tog] twice, k1, p2*; repeat from * to * to end of round—28 sts remain.

**Round 8:** *Ssk, k1, k2tog, p2*; repeat from * to * to end of round—20 sts remain.

**Round 9:** *K3tog, p2 *; repeat from * to * to end of round—12 sts remain.

*If desired, the k3tog can be worked as follow: s1, k2tog, psso.*

**Round 10:** *K1, p2tog*; repeat from * to * to end of round—8 sts remain.

To finish the hat, cut the yarn leaving a tail at least 8" (20 cm) long. Using a yarn needle, thread the tail through the remaining stitches and pass through the hole in the top of the hat to the inside. Pull the tail firmly to close the hole and weave the ends into the stitches on the inside of the hat to secure. Weave in all ends.

# Flower Power Hat

This pattern uses self-striping yarn in a simple stranded colorwork pattern. It makes you look like a genius of a knitter because even though you're only using two different yarns it appears as if you've changed colors all through the design. The dark background yarn makes a beautiful frame for the rainbow hue stripes of color. The pattern is a simple one that doesn't have any long floats on the back so it's easy to maintain even tension.

For stranded knitting, experienced knitters often use the "two handed" method: carry one color in the left hand and the other color in the right hand. It may take a bit of practice so if you're new to stranded knitting, take the time to read How To Knit With Two Colors below.

## HOW TO KNIT WITH TWO COLORS

To get used to colorwork knitting, make a practice swatch. Cast on 48 stitches (divisible by 12 which you'll see later is important) and join in the round. Begin by making a few rows of k2, p2 ribbing.

The hat is made of segments of 12 stitches that are repeated over and over around the hat (a total of eight times). The chart will show just a single segment of 12 stitches. Start reading the chart from the bottom right corner. The first round of knitting is represented by the squares at the bottom of the chart. The blue squares represent yarn A and the green squares represent yarn B. If you see a blue square (or two or three, etc.) then knit with yarn A. If you see a green square (or more) then knit with yarn B instead. Read the bottom line from right to left. After you complete the first 12 stitches then repeat line 1 from the chart over and over until you reach the BOR marker. When you finish knitting round 1 according to the chart then start back at the right side and read line 2 from right to left (repeating over and over until the end of the round).

The next challenge with stranded colorwork is what to do with the two strands. Honestly, it's pretty easy–hold yarn A (blue in photo) in your left hand and yarn B (gold in photo) in your right hand. The index fingers of each hand will do the heavy lifting, keeping tension on

### GAUGE

20 sts = 4" (10 cm) in stockinette stitch

22 sts = 4" (10 cm) in stranded colorwork pattern

### YARN

Yarn A: Medium weight smooth yarn, 55 yd (50 m)

Yarn B: Medium weight smooth, self striping yarn, 70 yd (64 m)

Shown:

Yarn A: Dream in Color *Classy*, 100% merino wool; 250 yd (230 m) per 4 oz (112 g) skein, color Purple Rain

Yarn B: Crystal Palace Yarn, *Mochi Plus*, 80% merino wool, 20% nylon; 95 yd (87 m) per 1.75 oz (50 g) ball, color #557, Autumn Rainbow

### NEEDLES AND NOTIONS

US size 8 (5 mm) 16" (41 cm) circular needle or size required to achieve gauge

US size 6 (4 mm) 16" (41 cm) circular needle (or two sizes smaller than size used to achieve gauge)

US size 8 (5 mm) double-pointed needles or size required to achieve gauge

Optional Magic Loop: above needle sizes in a circular needle at least 40" (101 cm) long.

Circular stitch marker

Yarn needle for weaving in ends

their respective yarns, and your thumbs and other fingers will have the job of holding the needles. To knit yarn B, insert the right needle into the stitch and use your right finger to make a loop around the needle and form a stitch (1). To knit yarn A, insert the right needle into the stitch and using your left finger to keep some tension on the yarn, move the needle up and over the yarn and then back toward you to make a loop and complete the stitch (2). As you change back and forth between the two colors, the unused yarn will make a horizontal line, or strand, across the back of your knitting.

Practice makes perfect—one of your hands is going to be inexperienced with holding yarn but before long it will feel like that hand actually belongs to your body. That's why it's a good idea to cast on a smaller number of stitches, join in the round, and use it not only to make a swatch but also to practice your technique. A final word about two-color knitting, and this is where practice is helpful: maintaining even tension is important. The tension in stranded knitting has a tendency to be tight because the strands on the back side are pulled too tightly, thereby making them too short. When you change from one color to another, stretch out the stitches on your right needle before you pull the new color across to begin knitting. This translates into a bit of slack in the new color and will help to maintain even, loose tension. Another trick I learned from my good friend Karen is to change the strands from hand to hand. At the start of the round, look to see which color is going to be used the most and change that color to your dominant hand which will do a better job of controlling the tension. One last bit of advice—smile! It helps with tight tension, honest.

1

2

Yarn strands float on the wrong side of the knitting.

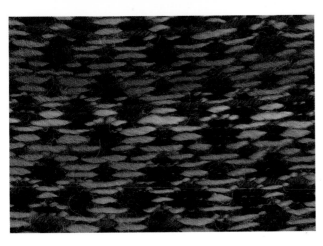

## FLOWER POWER HAT: Finished Size and Dimensions

| Finished Size | Hat Circumference | Finished Hat Height |
|---|---|---|
| Average Female Head: 19" (48.5 cm) to 21" (53.5 cm) | 17½" (44.5 cm) | 8" (20 cm) |

## FLOWER POWER HAT

The colorwork pattern is a multiple of 12 stitches which are represented by the detail color chart at right. If you want to change the size of the hat, do so by adding or subtracting stitches in a multiple of 12 (which equals about 2" [5 cm]). The height of the hat will need to be adjusted accordingly.

Using smaller circular needle and yarn A, cast on 96 stitches. Place BOR marker and join in the round being careful not to twist (see page 20).

**Round 1:** *K2, p2*; repeat from * to * to end of round.

Repeat round 1 for six more rounds or until the length from the cast-on edge is approximately 1½" (4 cm).

Change to larger needles, join yarn B and follow chart through row 30.

### SHAPE TOP

Continue to follow the chart but in addition to changing the colors, include the decreases as shown. If you are more comfortable with written directions then follow what is shown below. Change to DPNs when the stitches will no longer fit comfortably around the circular needle.

**Round 1:** *With yarn A, ssk, k1; with yarn B, k1; with yarn A, k4; with yarn B, k1; with yarn A, k1, k2tog*; repeat from * to * to end of round—80 sts remain.

**Round 2:** With yarn A, knit.

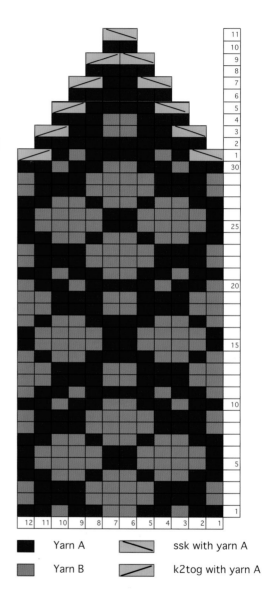

| Yarn A | ssk with yarn A |
|---|---|
| Yarn B | k2tog with yarn A |

**Round 3:** *With yarn A, ssk, k2; with yarn B, k2; with yarn A, k2, k2tog*; repeat from * to * to end of round—64 sts remain.

**Round 4:** *With yarn A, k3; with yarn B, k2; with yarn A, k3*; repeat from * to * to end of round.

Discontinue yarn B and finish hat with yarn A only.

**Round 5:** *Ssk, k4, k2tog*; repeat from * to * to end of round—48 sts remain.

**Round 6:** Knit.

**Round 7:** *Ssk, k2, k2tog*; repeat from * to * to end of round—32 sts remain.

**Round 8:** Knit.

**Round 9:** *Ssk, k2tog*; repeat from * to * to end of round—16 sts remain.

**Round 10:** Knit.

**Round 11:** *Ssk*; repeat from * to * to end of round—8 sts remain.

To finish the hat, cut the yarn leaving a tail at least 8" (20 cm) long. Using a yarn needle, thread the tail through the remaining stitches and pass through the hole in the top of the hat to the inside. Pull the tail firmly to close the hole and weave the ends into the stitches on the inside of the hat to secure.

To finish hat, weave in all ends and steam lightly.

# Abbreviations

Here is the list of standard abbreviations used for knitting. Until you can readily identify them, keep the list handy whenever you knit.

| | | | |
|---|---|---|---|
| 2-st RT | two-stitch right twist | p3tog | purl three together |
| 4-st RKC | four-stitch right knit cross | pf&b | purl front and back |
| 6-st RKC | six-stitch right knit cross | pm | place marker |
| BOR | beginning of round | psso | pass slipped stitch over |
| cm | centimeter | rm | remove marker |
| dpn(s) | double pointed needles | rs | right side |
| g | gram | ws | wrong side |
| inc | increase (lifted increase) | sl | slip |
| K, k | knit | sm | slip marker |
| k2tog | knit two together | ssk | slip, slip, knit |
| k3tog | knit three together | SSP | Slip Stitch Pattern |
| kf&b | knit front and back | st | stitch |
| LYS | local yarn shop | sts | stitches |
| m | meter | wyib | with yarn in back |
| M1L | make one left | wyif | with yarn in front |
| M1LP | make one left - purl | yo | yarnover |
| M1R | make one right | * * | repeat instructions between * as directed |
| M1RP | make one right - purl | | |
| P, p | purl | [ ] | repeat instructions enclosed by brackets as directed |
| p2tog | purl two together | | |